The Really Useful #EdTechBook
David Hopkins

REVIEWS FOR THE REALLY USEFUL #EDTECHBOOK

Steve Wheeler, Associate Professor of Learning Technology, Plymouth University:

> "The Really Useful #EdTechBook does exactly what it promises on its cover. It draws together a useful, diverse, eclectic set of visions and commentaries that together provide the reader with a lucid and comprehensive vista of educational technology. It traces the history of learning technology, catalogues the present state of play, and envisages the future. David Hopkins has done extremely well to gather this band of authors together, because they represent a vast amount of experience. Many have been at the forefront of development and innovation in their respective fields – in Further and Higher Education, and corporate training. The mix of academic, practical and theoretical offerings is a useful recipe book for any aspiring Learning Technologist."

Maren Deepwell, Chief Executive, Association for Learning Technology (ALT):

> "The Really Useful #EdTechBook is an insightful and thought-provoking read for anyone with an interest in the role of technology for learning, teaching and assessment today. Decision makers will find it a useful resource to gain a deeper understanding of the key issues involved. It does more than bring together a collection of interesting accounts from across Further and Higher Education, it demonstrates why open collaboration and knowledge exchange are key characteristics of those who successfully meet the challenges learning technology poses in a rapidly evolving landscape. You don't have to be a Learning Technologist to read this book, but you might wish you had more of their expertise at your side when you're finished."

Chrissi Nerantzi, Principal Lecturer in Academic CPD, Centre for Excellence in Learning and Teaching, Manchester Metropolitan University:

> "A very insightful and extensive collection of authentic accounts by practitioners who identify themselves as Learning Technologists in a variety of educational settings. This reminds us of the fast pace of change in this relatively new profession, the variety of roles and responsibilities as well as the passion of these individuals for supporting change, innovation and transformation in the digital age. Challenges and opportunities linked to professional identity, engagement and positioning are discussed."

> "As an Academic Developer in Higher Education, the book made me reflect on our professional relationship with Learning Technologists. Sue Beckingham in her chapter talks about the hybrid or blended professional for example, a mix between Learning Technologists and Academic Developer and the need to work together. David Walker and Sheila MacNeill take it one step further and raise an important question about the future of Learning Technologists: "Is there something fundamental that distinguishes Learning Technologists from educational developers? Do we still need both roles?" This question, I feel, could form the basis for further collaborative exploration between Learning Technologists, Academic Developers and the wider academic community

Neil Withnell, Associate Head Academic Enhancement, University of Salford:

> "It is a fascinating read and the title encapsulates the content of the book, I found it 'really useful' to read! The book is logical, insightful and provides the reader with a rich array of both personal experience and "tools" for use in education. The book will appeal to anyone who is interested in the use of technology in teaching and learning, highly recommended!"

ELECTRONIC DOWNLOAD

Many thanks for buying the printed paper copy of The Really Useful #EdTechBook.

There are two versions of the book available for you to download.

1. Scan the QR Code below with your smartphone and QR Code scanning App and download the PDF of the book. Alternatively you can type the shortened URL into your browser address bar and access the PDF that way.

http://goo.gl/OUUS7L

2. If you purchased the book through Amazon I have enrolled the title in Amazon 'Matchbook'. If Amazon has released Matchbook in your country then you are able to download the Kindle edition, for free, from Amazon.

CONTENTS

FOREWORD

CATHERINE CRONIN

"Dialogue cannot exist in the absence of a profound love for the world and for people." – Paulo Freire (1970)

Fires rage all around us in education today. As educators we face many familiar challenges, some of which have taken on new forms in recent years. What is the purpose of education, of further and higher education? Who should fund it? Who benefits? Where does learning happen? What role could and should technology play? Whose technology? At individual and institutional levels we face new challenges also. Among these: How best can we support learning in a landscape in which the boundaries between formal and informal learning are blurring? How do we support networked learning in the age of surveillance? How do we, and our students, effectively manage our data, our privacy, our digital identities?

Your work will no doubt be affected by many of these challenges – whatever your discipline, your education philosophy, your politics, or your role. And it is these challenges which inform much of the work of Learning Technologists.

The role of the Learning Technologist, particularly in Further and Higher Education, is relatively new and has evolved considerably in its short history (Conole, 2004; Hopkins, 2013; Oliver, 2002). This volume is authored by a diverse group of Learning Technologists who share their experiences of, and reflections on, their work. More importantly, however, they reveal much about their individual approaches to learning and teaching, to technology, to change, and to the future. The authors define themselves variously as Learning Technologist, Educational Developers, Digital Pedagogues, Lecturers, and Consultants. What unites them, however, is a collaborative and cross-disciplinary approach to curriculum development, and to professional and personal development. This is, at its simplest, a collection of articles by Learning Technologists. But the collection is also a live network of trusted and generous education professionals, each of whom describes their own learning as well as how they collaborate and support learning at their institutions. The Freirean spirit is evident here in the critical questioning and dialogic approach; in the joy and love of learning and of people.

There is plenty of polemic today about how technology could and should be used in education, and no shortage of criticism about how it is being used. This volume is neither. The collection is a resource for anyone interested in the use of technology in education and learning, authored by those responsible for the messy reality of "*managing, researching, supporting or enabling learning with the use of learning technology*" (ALT, 2010). The authors draw on their own experiences, supported both by research of their own as well as existing research in education, education technology, pedagogy, creativity, and innovation.

I am not a Learning Technologist. But, like many of the contributors to this collection, I consider myself an open educator, committed not just to open educational resources (as this book will be), but to open teaching, open thinking, and open learning. I invite you to dive into this volume, as I have done, with that spirit. Read about approaches that you agree with, as well as approaches with which you may disagree; read about work that is familiar to you, as well as work that is new to you. I join each of the authors in hoping that these contributions will form part of a wider and ongoing discussion about technology, learning, and the future of education.

REFERENCES

ALT. (2010). What is learning technology? [online] Available at: https://www.alt.ac.uk/about-alt/what-learning-technology

Conole, G. (2004). The role of learning technology practitioners and researchers in understanding networked learning. Proceedings of the Networked Learning Conference 2004, Lancaster University, UK.

Freire, P. (1970). Pedagogy of the Oppressed. London: Penguin.

Hopkins, D. (2013). What is a Learning Technologist? 1st edition.

Oliver, M. (2002). What do learning technologists do? Innovations in Education and Training International, 39(4), 245-252.

CITATION

Cronin, C. (2015). Foreword. In: Hopkins, D., ed., *The Really Useful #EdTechBook*, 1st ed. David Hopkins, pp.11-13.

INTRODUCTION

DAVID HOPKINS

eLearning Consultant, Warwick Business School.

@hopkinsdavid

http://www.dontwasteyourtime.co.uk

David has been involved in learning technology for 8 years, and has been writing about his journey and experiences since 2008. In his current role as an eLearning Consultant at Warwick Business School he continues to engage with academic and professional staff in and around the appropriate use of technology, to enhance learning experiences for both campus-based and distance learning students. David is a Fellow of the Higher Education Academy (HEA), a member of the Association for Learning Technology (ALT), and a holder of the Certified Membership of ALT (CMALT) qualification. In 2014 David was honoured by ALT as *"Highly Commended"* in the Learning Technologist of the Year Award.

I have often reflected on my role and on my own experiences as a Learning Technologist. These reflections have sometimes formed a blog post or a comment on someone else's blog. I've used the experience of reflection to self-check my work, my attitude, my approach, and my interactions with those I come into contact with. It's not an easy process and, once you start, is often one you can't easily stop. But it is good, and it has been extremely valuable.

This book is what happens when you can't stop thinking, analysing, reflecting, planning, growing, engaging, collaborating, writing, etc. This book is the result of many wonderful people who have helped me become the Learning Technologist that I am today, even if they don't realise it. This book is a result of the contacts I've made through the various online networks I inhabit: Twitter, LinkedIn, Google+, Facebook, blogs, etc. From these networks, and the connections made, has come a fuller understanding, appreciation, and passion for my work, my role, and the people I work with. This is quite easily summed up by saying:

> *A Learning Technologist cannot afford to be in an environment that does not challenge, innovate, collaborate, or engage them, just as a Learning Technologist cannot afford to not exhibit these qualities in the way they approach their work. (Hopkins, 2013)*

This book has been on my mind for some time. I've been making notes, talking with my peers, testing the water, writing a bit, and then ignoring it for ages. I then decided to sit down and do something about it. If you needed an elevator pitch for this book it is simply this - I want to generate discussion around learning and educational technology, in all its guises and different environments. It's about reflecting on our own experiences and practices and looking ahead, looking at what we think works, what we observe, and what we're going to do about it. This is what this book is - examples, experiences, exchanges, collaborations, and above all, knowledge.

My first foray into publishing my thoughts about being a Learning Technologist, and what one is, was to collate my series of blog posts called 'what is a Learning Technologist?' and various discussions around them into a single volume and offer it as an eBook. I didn't do it to try to make it a roaring commercial success but, as I had hoped, as a catalyst for the learning technology community to think and reflect on their own experiences and reflections as Learning Technologists or working with education or learning technologies. It seems to have worked as many blog posts have were spawned by some who read either my original blog posts or indeed the eBook – indeed, a couple of authors in this book are some of those who wrote about their own thoughts as Learning Technologists, hence the invite to write for The Really Useful #EdTechBook!

So why call ourselves Learning Technologists? It's not just because it's the label given to us by the HR department, or what was on the job specification when we applied. It is part of the wider understanding of how the role is used and viewed as part of the institutions' structure. For some the role grew from the type of role a 'demonstrator' had where they would prepare the classroom and classroom equipment for the teacher to use (a role the teacher can do themselves now due to the simplicity of the lectern-located PC and connected projector - no more overhead projectors for us, thank you). These demonstrators needed knowledge or understanding of the learning that would take place in the classroom in order to properly and appropriately set the classroom equipment up for the intended activity and outcome. For others the role came from IT Services where similar preparation and technical know-how was required, and from a more IT perspective than the demonstrator. These roles were often from the background of maintaining and supporting the equipment, not the teacher, thus the individual had excellent knowledge of the technology, but not necessarily how it could be used most effectively in a classroom activity.

As you can see from the contributors in this book, and their individual job titles - these are as varied and as individual as the people who fill the roles – this isn't just about Learning Technologists! I am currently labeled as an eLearning Consultant, one that fits the role and environment of a Business School. Labels and titles vary, such as Educational Developer (Sue Beckingham), Head of Technology Enhanced Learning (Dr David Walker), and Lecture in Learning Technology (Peter Reed) exist with the authors of this book; we even have a 'Captain' (Julian Stodd) here with us! Thankfully, some of us are at least still labeled as a Learning Technologist (Terese Bird, Wayne Barry), yet we share the similarities of the role and responsibilities, to a greater or lesser degree, highlighted by the definition from the Association for Learning Technology (ALT):

> *Learning technology is the broad range of communication, information and related technologies that can be used to support learning, teaching, and assessment. Learning Technologists are people who are actively involved in managing, researching, supporting or enabling learning with the use of learning technology. (ALT, 2010)*

Whether we engage in the actual day to day running and development of learning material, or are now the managers of teams of learning professionals doesn't matter as it is our affinity to the work and people we work with that counts. We have a passion for our work and it's our own understanding and progress that drives us. We are committed to our own personal learning (or 'Leisure Learning' as Inge de Warrd refers to it in her chapter) as well as having that commitment to furthering our experiences through our reading, blogging, research, conference activities, tweeting, etc. This is perfectly summed up by Sarah Horrigan (2012) in her post: 'on being a Learning Technologist... ':

> *A Learning Technologist is someone who can bridge the gap between learning and technology, can translate between the two fields, can spot opportunities and help make change happen within teaching practices and importantly, understands the context of learning in which they're placed.*

THE REALLY USEFUL #EDTECHBOOK

In this book you'll find experiences, expectations, reflections, and a few revelations, from leading and respected individuals working in the field of Learning or Educational Technology, from primary schools to further and higher education, from corporate and work-place learning to early-year schooling and museums. I invited these individuals as, through conversations and collaborations I've had with each of them over the last five or six years, I have learned to trust their judgment and perspectives. Each chapter presented here in this book is in the author's own words, their own experiences and perspective of learning technology and working with learning technology.

As Wayne Barry (2014) notes: *"if we can articulate what we do to ourselves, it makes it a little easier to articulate what we do to others."* This is why you have this book in your hands - you want to know more about learning technology and / or Learning Technologists. This is the sentiment that so many of us strive to achieve.

What about the actual use of technology? Adam Bellow, Outstanding Young Educator of the Year ISTE 2011, says, *"to define technology integration it's really using whatever resources you have to the best of your abilities."* (Edutopia, 2012). He goes on to quantify this statement by saying that:

Technology is a tool. It's what you do with that tool, what you can make, what you allow the students to make, that's really what [learning] technology is about. (Edutopia, 2012)

This is also wonderfully covered and explained by Martin Weller in his journal article about the 'pedagogy of abundance', a term I've only recently encountered. I've supported the appropriate and considered use of technology over the years, for any purpose not least where used in classrooms and/or distance learning. I now realise I've been supporting and advertising this 'pedagogy of abundance', where we are "*witnessing a fundamental change in the production of knowledge and our relationship to content*" (Weller, 2011). Are learning technology experts, these specialists in matching a learning need to a specific tool or system, entering a stage in education where it is as much about the transfer of digital skills and digital literacy, as it is about the specifics of the class subject or activity?

Has the onset of 'Bring Your Own Device' (BYOD) radically altered the need for a Learning Technologist – not only on how we do our job, but why, and for whom? Are we now closer aligned to the student and student experience than to the academic or learning? Anthony Chivetta wrote "*the need to know the capital of Florida died when my phone learned the answer*" (Chivetta, 2008), and that:

> *the students of tomorrow need to be able to think creatively: they will need to learn on their own, adapt to new challenges and innovate on-the-fly. As the realm of intellectual accessibility expands at amazing rates (due to greater global collaboration and access to information), students of tomorrow will need to be their own guides as they explore the body of information that is at their fingertips. My generation will be required to learn information quickly, use that information to solve new and novel problems, and then present those solutions in creative and effective ways. The effective students of tomorrow's world will be independent learners, strong problem solvers and effective designers." (Chivetta, 2008)*

Remember, Chivetta is not some experienced leader or researcher in education practices; when he said this he was a teenager in a US college – and his words still reverberate around the world of learning and technology today, especially when you talk about mobile or BYOD learning initiatives. We could argue that those of us involved in learning and educational technology also need to be as adaptable, as flexible, as independent, and as open to new ideas and approaches as the students we see in our classrooms or lecture theatres. You could also therefore argue that we need to be even *more* adaptable or *more* flexible than this (as Mike McSharry writes in his chapter here), that we need to be looking to the next cohort of students, see what they are currently doing with technology in colleges or schools, see how we can capture and encourage *their* learning in ways *they* favour. Indeed, what about looking even further forward to younger students? Observe the patterns in their learning and use of technology so that, when they reach us, in HE, FE, or the work place, we're ready for them with 'modern', up-to-date learning styles?

Everyone in this book shares this same sentiment, despite our varied backgrounds and roles - we don't force a tool or a technology on to a situation or solution, we critically evaluate the required, desired outcome or learning opportunity and look at the tools we know and have experience of … then we suggest possible solutions.

More importantly, if we don't know something, we go find out!

Thank you.

REFERENCES:

ALT, (2010). What is Learning Technology? [online] Available at: https://www.alt.ac.uk/about-alt/what-learning-technology [Accessed 28 Jul. 2014].

Barry, W. (2014). The Stories that Learning Technologists tell [Blog] The Accidental Technologist. Available at: http://www.waynebarry.com/blog/?p=914 [Accessed 31 Jul. 2014].

Chivetta, A. 2008. 21st Century Education: Thinking Creatively. Anthony Chivetta, [blog] 22 Jan 2008, Available at: http://chivetta.org/2008/01/22/21st-century-education-thinking-creatively/ [Accessed: 1 Dec 2013].

Edutopia, (2012). An Introduction to Technology Integration. [video] Available at: https://www.youtube.com/watch?v=d59eG1_Tt-Q [Accessed 5 Aug. 2014].

Hopkins, D. (2013). What is a Learning Technologist (part 9): Ignorance is bliss? [Blog] Technology

Enhanced Learning Blog. Available at: http://www.dontwasteyourtime.co.uk/elearning/ignorance-is-bliss/ [Accessed 10 Aug. 2014].

Horrigan, S. (2012). On being a Learning Technologist... and farewell!. [Blog] Learning Technologies. Available at: http://learningtechnologiesteam.blogspot.co.uk/2012/12/on-being-learning-technologist-and.html [Accessed 31 Jul. 2014]

Weller, Martin (2011). A pedagogy of abundance. Spanish Journal of Pedagogy, 249 pp. 223–236. Available at: http://oro.open.ac.uk/28774/2/BB62B2.pdf [Accessed 17 November 2014]

CITATION

Hopkins, D. (2015). Introduction. In: Hopkins, D., ed., *The Really Useful #EdTechBook*, 1st ed. David Hopkins, pp.15-21.

"…AND WHAT DO YOU DO?" CAN WE EXPLAIN THE UNEXPLAINABLE?

WAYNE BARRY

Learning Technologist, Canterbury Christ Church University.

@HeyWayne

http://www.waynebarry.com

Wayne Barry is a Learning Technologist at Canterbury Christ Church University, with special research interests in social media, e-portfolios and learning spaces. He teaches on the University's PGCAP programme and has acted as a Teaching Assistant on the 'e-Learning and Digital Cultures' MOOC for the University of Edinburgh. He is an Associate Fellow with the Higher Education Academy (HEA) and a member of the British Computer Society (BCS). He is currently undertaking a Doctorate in Education (EdD).

Unlike other occupations, the job title of Learning Technologist does not elicit the same kind of shared, universal understanding of most other professions, such as teacher, doctor or solicitor. We find that even within our own communities of practice that it is a little difficult to explain or define what it is that we do. Furthermore, as Browne & Beetham (2010) note in their report, there are "*varying nuances*" between the terms 'learning technology' and 'educational technology'. Thus, exasperating an already complex and divergent field that is still trying to make sense of the confusing and contradictory nature surrounding the terminology and interpretation of names and job titles that have been generated through the likes of definitions, lists, and socially constructed discourses.

In this book chapter, through my own personal experience, I will try and derive some sense of meaning behind those troublesome terms and consider how this impacts on how we, as learning professionals, are perceived from within and outside of our professional communities and institutions.

PROLOGUE

You know how it is, you've been invited to a social gathering, the drinks are flowing nicely; the nibbles are going down a storm; and the conversation is light and convivial. Suddenly, someone asks you the very question that you have been hoping and praying would not get asked: "...and what do you do?". The corner of your mouth begins to spasm and you begin to blink more than is entirely necessary as you try to form those enigmatic and arcane words that are only known to those of us who share the same affiliation, the same vocation: "I...I...I'm a Learning Technologist". That's when it happens, snap, the incantation has been cast and you watch as the head of the person, who asked that dreaded question, begins to slowly tilt to one side like an inquisitive bird and their sharp, intelligent eyes begin to glaze over as they try to comprehend the significance of the statement you have just made. You watch helplessly as their nice and compartmentalised world comes crashing down around their feet as they try to come to terms with the enormous, earth-shattering, life-changing piece of information that you have passed on to them.

I may well have over-embellished the above scenario a tad too much. But, the important point to consider is that unlike other occupations, such as *teacher*, *mechanic*, *plumber*, *doctor* and *solicitor*, the term 'learning' or 'educational' technologist does not elicit the same kind of shared, universal understanding of most other occupations. Even within our own communities of practice, we find it a little difficult to explain or define what it is that we do.

In this chapter, I should like to focus upon those terms 'learning' / 'educational' technologist and try and derive some sense of meaning behind those terms. It soon becomes clear to me that given the complex and divergent nature of our field, it is almost impossible to come up with a nice and tidy definition, though others have clearly tried – how successful they have been very much depends upon your own personal, professional and institutional context.

IN THE BEGINNING…

When I first joined Canterbury Christ Church University in 1989 (though it was a college back then), I worked in a small IT department of four people; my role was that of an IT Technician. By 1996, the college had become a university college and I was now working in a small unit called *TiTLe* (Technology in Teaching and Learning) as Information and Communications Technology (ICT) Development Officer doing a lot of web and multimedia based development of content and resources. This small unit sat squarely within the IT department, which, by then, had grown considerably. In July 1999, I left Canterbury Christ Church to work in the private sector as a senior web developer.

In August 2006, I found myself returning to Canterbury Christ Church University to take up the position of Learning Technologist. This role, crucially, did not sit within the IT department, but within a learning and teaching directorate, thus emphasising that the role was very much situated around learning, teaching, assessment, professional development and the student experience and not just about computers, technology and the Internet.

It was in the previous year, 2005 that I first became conscious of the term 'Learning Technologist' when I saw a job advert in one of the popular broadsheet newspapers. Upon reading the job description, I was immediately struck how similar it was to that of my previous role of an ICT Development Officer, which had all the "hallmarks" of a Learning Technologist and an Educational Developer, though these phrases were not known to me in 1996.

DEFINING THE UNDEFINABLE?

Like most Learning Technologists, we all have some kind of anecdote or 'war story' where we have gone to a social gathering and the conversation has weaved its way towards the inevitable discussion around our respective occupations only to be greeted with a glazed look or, if we were very lucky, someone might say "*Oh!*

That's interesting!' I have known colleagues to deliberately subjugate the conversation with alternative job titles like *IT trainer, eLearning consultant,* or *teacher* as a means to avoid the inevitable long-winded and tortuous explanation as to what a Learning Technologist is and what they do – whilst this can be seen as an opportunity to raise awareness of our field to those who are not familiar with it; it does fill me with dread as I replay in my head the typical lines of discussion that these kinds of conversations tend to take.

Incidentally, I have one colleague who recounts the story that upon being asked about his job, replied that he made the McVitie's *Hobnobs* biscuit, rather than declare himself as a Learning Technologist.

However, it wasn't until I embarked on a Doctorate in Education (EdD) in March 2013 that I began to seriously consider my role as a Learning Technologist. The EdD is a professional doctorate and all of the doctoral students within that programme of study are actively encouraged by the tutors to try and situate educational theories and philosophies within their own professional practices and contexts. So, for me, the EdD has very much been aligned towards my own professional practice and identity of being a Learning Technologist.

It soon became clear to me that my personal knowledge of being a Learning Technologist was quite limited and superficial. I knew that the *Association of Learning Technology* (ALT) in the UK, defines learning technology as:

> *...the broad range of communication, information and related technologies that can be used to support learning, teaching, and assessment. (ALT, 2014)*

But, I was quick to discover that in the US, the internationally renowned professional body called the *Association for Educational Communications and Technology* (AECT) offers an alternative definition, but relating to 'educational technology', and describes it as:

> *...the study and ethical practice of facilitating learning and improving*

performance by creating, using, and managing appropriate technological processes and resources. (AECT, 2008)

Both definitions are quite short and succinct making references to "*supporting*" or "*facilitating*" learning through "*related*" or "*appropriate*" technologies. The AECT definition, for example, has gone through many iterations since its' inception in the 1970s and as such have caused a number of commentators to pick up on the phrase "*improving performance*" that has crept into the latest iteration of the definition (Hlynka & Jacobsen, 2009), which seems to be bound around notions of performativity and monitoring. Furthermore, other scholars like Paul Saettler (1968, cited in Hawkridge, 1976:8), perceives educational technology as "*the practical art of using scientific knowledge about education*". Whereas Derek Rowntree (1982) provides an argument that education technology "*is concerned with the design and evaluation of curricula and learning experiences and with the problems of implementing and renovating them*" (p.1).

The deeper I dug into the research literature around 'learning' and 'educational' technology, the bigger the black hole of confusion and contradiction that began to emerge. In the report *The Positioning of Educational Technologists in Enhancing the Student Experience* by Browne & Beetham (2010), they note that there are "varying nuances" (p.6) between the terms 'learning technology' and 'educational technology'. It was becoming patently clear to me that a number of practitioners, scholars and researchers believe that:

> *Just as it is difficult to define educational technology, so it is almost impossible to identify an educational technologist. (Lawless & Kirkwood, 1976:54)*

And more recently:

> *But any agreed definition of an educational technologist remains elusive, and is usually framed by a list of activities or roles. (Browne & Beetham, 2010:12)*

Other commentators like Norman MacKenzie (1976:5) asks "*[i]s it a mystery, an art or a science?*" or is it something else "*sheltering for protection under a somewhat pretentious title*"? Luppicini (2005:103) reports that the field of educational technology "*shares many of the same struggles*" as the social and applied social sciences in terms of "*defining itself and substantiating its foundations*". He goes on to argue that some of the issues and challenges in defining educational technology tends to be "*clouded by discourses taking place outside the field*" (*ibid.*, p.103). Whilst Professor David Hawkridge, the first Director of the Open University's Institute of Educational Technology (IET), is also keen to caution us that:

> *It is very tempting to propose a cast-iron definition of educational technology, from which it might then be possible to identify the boundaries and constraints of this paper. To use such a definition, however, is to risk implying that the field is in a static state, whereas it is dynamic and shifting constantly: 'a moving target', according to Amsey and Dahl (1973). (Hawkridge, 1976:8)*

So where does all this leave me? If the experts cannot adequately articulate what a Learning Technologist is, how could I be expected to do the same? Little did I know that this was just the very tip of a very large iceberg…

THE CASE OF THE "EMPTY SHELL"

Learning technology in the UK Higher Education (HE) sector can trace its' roots as far back as the late 1960s and, in particular, with the creation of the Open University. A number of articles, dating back to 1976, featured in the *British Journal of Educational Technology* (BJET) had spoken about the work of the OU's educational technologists, as they were known back then. The articles also make reference to educational technologists being sporadically located in other UK universities, though it is widely acknowledge that the OU had the highest concentration of educational technologists at the time.

However, the really big expansion in learning technology and Learning Technologists came in 1997 with the influential *National Committee of Inquiry into*

Higher Education (NCIHE, 1997), otherwise known as the *Dearing Report.* Conversely, in the US, educational technology can trace its' roots even further back to around the 1910s to the 1920s which rose out of the educational psychology and audio-visual traditions.

So given that learning, *albeit*, educational technology has been around in the UK for over 50 years, why is it that I am still known as "*The Blackboard Guy*" and that I must work in the university's IT department? When I first started out as a Learning Technologist, it use to annoy me intensely that I was pigeonholed against a particular type of technology especially as my role encompasses so much more. For a lot of academic and professional services staff, they cannot (or will not?) distinguish between learning technology and information technology. It is all technology as far as they are concerned. It all amounts to the same thing. Anything remotely to do with technology has to sit within an IT department or an Audiovisual (AV) Services unit, not a learning and teaching directorate. It creates an interesting set of tensions where the Learning Technologist finds themselves stuck in a kind of "*no man's land*" as a "*displaced professional*" located between Academia and Professional Services whilst grappling with some form of "*dissociative professional identity disorder*".

Hawkridge's cautionary note about proposing a "*cast-iron definition*" of learning technology reminds me of David Baume's (2012a, 2012b) notion of the "*empty shell definition*", which he discusses within the concept of digital literacy, he says:

> *It has both the advantage and the disadvantage of being an 'empty shell' account, albeit a shell with three compartments – the capabilities for 'living', 'learning' and 'working' – waiting to be filled. Both its advantage and its disadvantage is that it needs to be developed before it can be applied to policy, strategy and practice for course design, teaching, learning and assessment. (ibid., 2012a:6).*

He elaborates further, by suggesting that:

> *The wish to use empty shell definitions is understandable – they push the*

responsibility of populating the definition on to the particular users, and thus increase local ownership. (ibid., 2012b).

On the subject of creating definitions, Martin Weller (2011) argues that it "*should probably be resisted, and [at] best interpreted as a shorthand term*" and warns that "*such tight definitions can end up excluding elements that should definitely be included or including ones that seem incongruous*" (Well, 2011. p.5).

If we begin to really look at the roles of the Educational Technologist and Learning Technologist as they were originally conceived in the UK in the 1970s and 1990s respectively, there is a sense that an Educational Technologist was much more concerned with systems (i.e. products), whilst the emphasis for the Learning Technologist was more around pedagogy (i.e. processes). However, looking at the 'job specification' for the OU educational technologists in Northcott's (1976:13,15) paper, one is struck by how similar their role is to most contemporary Learning Technologists. Indeed, elements of the role can be found in the Beetham, Jones & Gornall (2001:29-31) report, whereby the authors had identified 11 distinct roles that included some form of learning technology activity, to a lesser or greater extent. This adds an extra layer of confusion, as it soon becomes apparent that Learning Technologists in other institutions may not necessarily perform the same roles as myself or, indeed, with others. Furthermore, if we do share the same roles, then they may not necessarily be called a Learning or Educational Technologist.

This is all very well and interesting, but where does this leave me now? How closer am I to understanding my role much more? We have tried to define our role; we have attempted to list those characteristics that are pertinent to our role, but to little or no avail. This linguistic genealogical investigation has not really helped me to distinguish those "*varying nuances*" that are supposed to exist between 'learning technology' and 'educational technology'; let alone trying to articulate to others as to what a Learning Technologist is and what they are supposed to do because it doesn't necessarily mean the same thing in other institutions. Saying that I make the McVitie's *Hobnobs* biscuit is growing increasingly attractive to me, but is there another way at looking at this? Is there another way in which I, and many of my peers, are able to make some sense of this 'troublesome terminology'?

CULTURALLY BIASED OR CULTURALLY SITUATED?

In a Twitter conversation (Barry, 2013) between myself, David Hopkins and a number of other learning and teaching professionals, I asked the question: "*Is there a difference between a 'Learning Technologist' and an 'Educational Technologist'?*" This question was prompted by the "*varying nuances*" between the terms that Browne & Beetham (2010:6) had alluded to, which were really beginning to niggle away at me. During the Twitter conversation, Lindsay Jordan, a Senior Lecturer in Learning and Teaching at the University of the Arts London, suggested that the terms were "*socially constructed*" and were situated within a political and historical context.

To some extent educational technology is partially explained as being a "*culturally biased phenomenon*" (Hlynka, 2003) with the current discourse, far from being universal, seemingly orientated towards a "*unique United States*" perspective which tends to be wrapped up in a "*particular idea of progress*" (i.e. making education quicker, simpler and more efficient) (*ibid.*, 2003). So, from a UK perspective, it should be noted that during the late 1990s, the language and discourse moved away from one of "*education*" to one of "*learning*", thus shifting the emphasis towards a more student-centred approach. In 2014, we find that, once again, the language has changed back to "*education*" to reflect the "*commodification*" of education and the transformation of students from "*learners*" to "*consumers*". Saettler (2004, [1990]) suggested that educational technology had an "*historical function*", but I think we can argue that educational technology has an increasingly "*economic-political function*".

Luppicini (2005), like Lindsay Jordan, argues that the problem with educational technology is that 'hard' sciences (like engineering and physics) and 'soft' sciences (like sociology and psychology) perceive the term "*technology*" in different ways, thus creating confusion around the term's usage (p.104). For engineers and technicians, technology is perceive to be the "*process of material construction based on systematic engineering knowledge of how to design artifacts*" (*ibid.*, p.104). But, for social science scholars, technology "*refers to material construction uses as well as the intellectual and social contexts*" (*ibid.*, p.104).

So, it does come as a bit of surprise to me to discover that most Learning Technologists "*are rather bored by issues of terminology*", according to Browne & Beetham's (2010:25) report. It would seem that I am in the minority here and that for most of my peers, they would rather conceive and articulate our roles in terms of *areas of activities, core knowledge and professional values which are akin to the precepts of the UK Professional Standards Framework (UKPSF)* (HEA, 2011) as defined by the UK's Higher Education Academy (HEA), thus grounding our role within a more professional and academic context.

CONCLUSION

When I started to investigate my role of a Learning Technologist as part of my EdD, I didn't realise that I was going to stumble across a very rich, vibrant and complex field that constantly shifted to reflect the economic, political, cultural and technological changes and challenges of the day.

Like Oliver (2002), Browne & Beetham (2010), Weller (2011), and many others before and after them, I have a feeling that we will not have a nice, neat, tidy definition or even a nice, neat, tidy list of comparisons. Our respective roles, be it 'educational' or 'learning' technologist, is far too complex, far too diverse and far too messy to try and encapsulate it in a bland, "*empty shell*" definition. What we can do is to look at our respective roles and to begin to construct a set of features, characteristics and properties pertaining to them and look for commonality; but more crucially, look for the differences. Once we feel confident that we know and understand our roles, then we will be able to answer the question "…and what do you do?" with more ease, more confidence and self-assurance.

In all ways, I am very proud to be a Learning Technologist, but more importantly, I am very proud to call myself a Learning Technologist with the wonderful opportunity it has given me to work with some incredible people on some amazing projects. Our challenge is how we engage with ourselves, our institutions and the wider public and make them aware as to who were are, what we are and what we do.

REFERENCES

Association for Educational Communications and Technology (AECT). (2008). "Definition". In: Januszewski, A & Molenda, M. (eds.). *Educational Technology: A definition with commentary*. New York: Lawrence Erlbaum Associates.

Association for Learning Technology (ALT). (2014). *What is Learning Technology?*. Oxford, England: Association for Learning Technology. Available at: http://www.alt.ac.uk/about-alt/what-learning-technology [Accessed 26.8.2014].

Barry, W. (2013). *Is there a difference between a "learning technologist" and an "educational technologist"? #LTHE #edtech*. [Twitter] 7.11.2013. Available at: https://twitter.com/HeyWayne/status/398476849476415488 [Accessed 17.10.2014].

Baume, D. (2012a). "Digital Literacy and Fluency: SEDA initiatives supporting an enlightened approach to Academic Development in the field". *Educational Developments*, 13(2), pp. 6-10. Available at: http://www.seda.ac.uk/resources/files/publications_129_Ed%20Devs%2013.2%20v3%20%28FINAL%29.pdf [Accessed 23.2.2014].

Baume, D. (2012b). "Digital literacies and digital fluency – a process of development? ". *SEDA SIG* blog, 14.11.2012. Available at: http://sedasig.wordpress.com/2012/11/14/digital-literacies-and-digital-fluency-a-process-of-development/ [Accessed 23.2.2014].

Beetham, H., Jones, S. & Gornall, L. (2001). *Career Development of Learning Technology Staff: Scoping Study Final Report for the JISC CALT*. Bristol, England: University of Plymouth, University of Bristol. Available at: http://www.jisc.ac.uk/uploaded_documents/cdss_final_report_v8.doc [Accessed 26.8.2014].

Browne, T. & Beetham, H. (2010). *The positioning of educational technologists in enhancing the student experience*. Report funded by The Higher Education Academy under their Call4: Enhancing Learning and Teaching through the use of Technology. Oxford, England: Association for Learning Technology (ALT) and The Higher Education Academy (HEA). Available at: http://repository.alt.ac.uk/831/ [Accessed 23.11.2013].

Hawkridge, D.G. (1976). "Next Year, Jerusalem! The Rise of Educational Technology". *British Journal of Educational Technology*, 7(1), pp. 7–30. Available at: http://dx.doi.org/10.1111/j.1467-8535.1976.tb00185.x [Accessed 24.11.2013].

Higher Education Academy (HEA). (2011). *UK Professional Standards Framework (UKPSF) for Teaching and Supporting Learning in Higher Education*. York, England: Higher Education Academy. Available at: https://www.heacademy.ac.uk/sites/default/files/downloads/UKPSF_2011_English.pdf [Accessed 29.8.2014].

Hlynka, D. (2003). "The Cultural Discourses of Educational Technology: A Canadian Perspective". *Educational Technology*, July-August. 41-45. Available at: http://www.umanitoba.ca/centres/ukrainian_canadian/hlynka/papers/Cultural_Discourses.pdf [Accessed 24.11.2013].

Hlynka, D. & Jacobsen, M. (2009). "What is educational technology, anyway? A commentary on the new AECT definition of the field". *Canadian Journal of Learning and Technology*, 35(2). Available at: http://www.cjlt.ca/index.php/cjlt/article/view/527/260 [Accessed 30.10.2013].

Lawless, C. & Kirkwood, A. (1976). "Training the Educational Technologist". *British Journal of Educational Technology*, 7(1), pp. 54–60. Available at: http://dx.doi.org/10.1111/j.1467-8535.1976.tb00188.x [Accessed 24.11.2013].

Luppicini, R. (2005). "A Systems Definition of Educational Technology in Society". *Educational Technology & Society*, 8(3), pp. 103-109. Available at: http://www.ifets.info/journals/8_3/10.pdf [Accessed 24.11.2013].

MacKenzie, N. (1976). "A Crisis of Identity". *British Journal of Educational Technology*, 7(1), pp. 4–6. Available at: http://dx.doi.org/10.1111/j.1467-8535.1976.tb00184.x [Accessed 24.11.2013].

Northcott, P. (1976). "The Institute of Educational Technology, the Open University: Structure and Operations, 1969-1975". *Innovations in Education & Training International*, 13(4), pp. 11-24. Available at: http://dx.doi.org/10.1080/1355800760130403 [Accessed 25.8.2014].

Oliver, M. (2002) "What do Learning Technologists do?". *Innovations in Education and Teaching International*, 39(4), pp. 245-252. Available at: http://dx.doi.org/10.1080/13558000210161089 [Accessed 21.10.2013].

Rowntree, D. (1982). *Educational Technology in Curriculum Development*. 2nd Edition. London, England: Harper and Row.

Saettler, P. (1968). *A History of Instructional Technology*. New York, NY: McGraw-Hill.

Saettler, P. (2004, [1990]). *The Evolution of American Educational Technology*. 2nd Edition. Greenwich, CT: Information Age Publishing.

Weller, M. (2011). *The Digital Scholar: How technology is transforming scholarly practice*. London, England: Bloomsbury Academic. Available at: http://nogoodreason.typepad.co.uk/files/thedigitalscholar.pdf [Accessed 17.8.2014].

CITATION

Barry, W. (2015). "…and what do you do?" Can we explain the unexplainable?. In: Hopkins, D., ed., *The Really Useful #EdTechBook*, 1st ed. David Hopkins, pp.23-34.

WHY WE DO WHAT WE DO

ZAK MENSAH

Head of Transformation, Bristol Museums, Galleries & Archives

@zakmensah

http://www.zakmensah.co.uk

I help people to use technology and transform how they run services. I regularly write on my personal blog zakmensah.co.uk, I speak at events across the UK about strategy and getting stuff done on the web. I have worked for two Universities and am currently working for the largest museum service in the South West with over 1 million visitors per year. I am based in Bristol. You're welcome to get in touch.

Using technology is a given in nearly all walks of life within education. Yet understanding WHY we're planning a digital intervention and understanding how to best plan, build and test our methods is overlooked. In this chapter I'll answer how to plan and review your use of technology.

WHY WE DO WHAT WE DO

I help people to use technology. That's what I tell folks who ask me about my line of work. Over the years I've worked with countless people and organisations to make sense of what seemed to come naturally to me as a teenager. I first recall using the Internet at my secondary school, which had one Internet-enabled computer. The first website I ever visited was about WWF (World Wrestling Federation) wrestlers. And every year since then there has been ever more to be curious about. It's a combination of people and the technology built by other people that I never tire of.

I enjoy 'helping people' and technology is the vehicle that allows me to do it.

That's a brief history of why I ended up working in the lane that I do today. I became a Learning Technologist back in 2006 before I even knew what the meaning of the job title was. People, technology, and curiosity have kept me in gainful employment going on for ten years. My job titles may have changed but my purpose hasn't. I want to help you know how to get to the route of your issue.

START

One of the not-so-secret secrets of our profession is that many Learning Technologists started doing lots of this stuff before it really was a profession with titles and 'best practices'. We saw something that looked fun to tackle and we dived in. If you haven't already I suggest you do the same. Nobody using your VLE area? Find out why. A colleague knows more than you about how to update a Wikipedia entry? Ask them to show you how.

There is no skipping the path to getting better other than time and practice.

HAVE A PLAN

Most people tinker around the edges with using technology, both in their personal lives and at work. Enforced use of technology is the default for many of you. However you always need a plan once you get bored of tinkering. I call my plans 'roadmaps' because it sounds semi serious yet way more fun than a dull strategy document. Plus, when you take a road trip, you have a final destination but normally it's fine to find your own way to the end. There is always more than one direction for you to travel in. You can see an example of our 2015-18 digital roadmap *(1)* which is publicly viewable and uses the free online service Trello to collect and assign tickets. We split each activity into a SMART objective and it lives in a list such as 2015-16 or 'done' when completed for review. Sharing our roadmap in such a way helps all our stakeholders see what our priorities are and even gets external public and servcies getting in touch to offer help. I highly recommend you do the same. I know some people worry about sharing but I think it's helpful, especially when using public money.

In August 2014 I wrote that I typically sound childlike *(2)* in my enquiry of a plan:

- You want to use the exact same approach as last time? WHY?
- Were there complaints? And if so. WHY?
- WHY can't we do this differently?
- WHY are we committing?
- WHY, if we're so busy, would you want us to do this?
- WHY can't I say no?

I want us to be as clear as possible that we're focused on the core reason for us to start a new project. Asking WHY really helps all of us refine our proposals. Once we know WHY we're doing something it's a lot easier to enjoy the ride!

I guess asking WHY a lot is the same as a IF / THEN / ELSE maybe process map. Once I have asked WHY enough and got to the root I have the makings of a roadmap.

In recent years there has been a push towards digital in all areas as there is a belief that it will save you money or make you money; hence all those interactive whiteboards, websites, and digital folks bogging down the balance sheets. For example I lean towards freely available resources, tools and free advice to get me going. It's from reading blogs such as David Hopkins' Don't Waste Your Time *(3)* that I became convinced that I could also add value to the sector of education and technology. This is why I took up speaking at any event that would have me talking about my experiences and problems. One of the things I find useful about speaking is that it forces me to challenge my rationale either through the writing or being challenged during my talk. I have recently started to blog too as a way of sharing like David and many others too. I don't have all the answers of course!

EDGES

Constraints. I used to think having constraints was a hindrance until I discovered that constraints are actually to our benefit and are simply "edges" for us to work within. With thousands of options for using technology at our disposal, having the odd constraint rules out much of the unnecessary. Craig Mod thinks of edges as a way to "*make the unconsumable, consumable*" *(4)*. Should you spend lots of time learning how to code? Well that depends if your target audience need you to know. How do you know what your audience needs? You find out who they are and ask them of course! For example very common 'edges' are time, resource and money. You have a finite budget, resource and a deadline. These help me shape how far I can go with any proposed solution. I can deliver a one page website if you only give me a day, no problem. These 'edges' are my scope and scale.

DISCOVERY

Find your edges quickly by completing a discovery phase. The smart folks at Government Digital Services define a discovery phase *(5)* as: "*What are the needs of your users? What services currently meet those? How are they performing? What technological or policy related constraints might there be?*" This is a critical and very insightful process to do within your area of work. When you know the answers to these questions you should feel a weight off your shoulders as you can turn your back on much of the Internet and technology, methods, etc. that suddenly have become out of reach. Understanding user needs is the single most critical aspect of our area of work. Furthermore, often you cannot pretend to represent your user. This means that although you are very experienced, your assumption of your user needs may be the biggest problem. You need to test your assumptions all the time.

I regularly work with people on projects that skip the discovery phase and the reason I'm often involved is because the product or service is underperforming or not meeting the expectations of the project team. No wonder if you decided you knew better. There are exceptions. Jared Spool writes in 'Actually, you might be your user:' *(6)*:

> *Self Design only works in those instances when you are the user and there's a lot of users just like you, using it the way you use it. If you are not in that situation, you will likely need to resort to an alternative style for making your design decisions. But if you are in that situation, then you*

may, in fact, be your own user and that's a good thing.

GATHERING INSIGHTS

I'm always surprised at how few people try to measure their use of technology. When I was supporting a VLE the staff would rarely monitor how many of their students looked at any of the resource they produced which must have taken them a long time to produce. I learned early that just because you build it wouldn't mean they'd come and use your services or resources. Helping people get insights is a key part of our role. There are lots of things you can measure including the number of views, downloads, completed surveys etc. In my current role we use a range of metrics to gather our insights and have taken four core Key performance indicators taken from Government Digital Services: cost per transaction, user satisfaction, completion rate and digital take-up *(7)*. For example at the museum we monitor satisfaction for our exhibitions using a simple 1-5 scale. We then benchmark the figure with our expectation based on previous similar exhibitions. We expect at least 80-95% satisfaction. Anything lower and we can dig into the comments to see if there are insights about the cause.

Once you have a range of collectable data and processes, you'll be able to make better-informed decisions in workplace and your chosen learning environments. The whole exercise should only take a day to set up but will give you and your colleague's helpful insights forever more. Setting this kind of activity running is one of my favourite aspects of my role.

CONCLUSION

I can let you into a little secret, I don't know everything about people and technology and this make me feel vulnerable. I don't know how to build an Application Programming Interface (API), I'm not the best coder and I don't know with certainty what technology will be the next big thing. I do know that even if I were to know, there will be another 100 topics that would make me feel like I don't know anything about the space we work in. Yet once I became comfortable being vulnerable I started to love what I do a lot more. That is fine by me. Remember now that technology has invaded our homes as well as our offices and that this technology space is a pretty exciting area of work to be in for the next few decades. Don't let the fact that technology is always changing cloud your vision and stop you from getting started. Change is constant but being helpful is always wanted and a large part of why we do what we do.

Go forth and be curious.

NOTES

1. Bristol Museums, Galleries & Archives digital roadmap https://trello.com/b/j6UN2Ivc/bmga-digital-roadmap-2014-2018

2. Zak Mensah. Not childish but childlike. http://zakmensah.co.uk/2014/08/01/not-childish-but-childlike

3. David Hopkins. Don't Waste Your Time blog.. http://www.dontwasteyourtime.co.uk

4. Craig Mod. Unbindings and Edges http://craigmod.com/sputnik/unbinding

5. Government Digital Services. http://gov.uk/service-manual/phases/discovery.html

6. Jared Spool. http://uie.com/articles/self_design

7. Government Digital Services. http://gov.uk/service-manual/measurement/other-kpis.html

CITATION

Mensah, Z. (2015). Why we do what we do. In: Hopkins, D., ed., *The Really Useful #EdTechBook*, 1st ed. David Hopkins, pp.35-40.

THE STRUCTURE AND ROLES OF LEARNING TECHNOLOGISTS WITHIN HIGHER EDUCATION INSTITUTIONS

PETER REED

Lecturer (Learning Technology), University of Liverpool

@reedyreedles

http://thereeddiaries.blogspot.co.uk

Peter is a Lecturer with a particular focus on Technology Enhanced Learning, based within the Faculty of Health & Life Sciences at the University of Liverpool. His main research interests are eLearning Pedagogy, eAssessment, Social Media, and Open Education.

INTRODUCTION

In his opening chapter to the book 'Digital Technology and the Contemporary University', Neil Selwyn attempts to move beyond the rhetoric of the '*digital university*' and discusses the hype, hope and fear of digital technologies within Higher Education (Selywn, 2014, p7). With such significant technological advances in recent years, he draws attention to the great expectations placed upon technology to disrupt the status quo amongst higher education institutions (HEIs), and contrasts the typical utopian and dystopian (or 'booster' and 'doomster') views that dominate technological developments.

This I believe, sets the tone nicely for the introduction to the Learning Technologist (LT) - a role that emerged to make sense of the messiness, and provide an expert view on when, where and how digital technologies might be effectively introduced to support and enhance all aspects of learning, teaching and assessment (LTA).

WHAT IS A LEARNING TECHNOLOGIST?

So what is a Learning Technologist anyway? For years I've struggled to define what I do when speaking with 'Muggles' - you know, those that don't posses our magical abilities. I've jokingly referred to the Friends sitcom character Chandler Bing in that nobody, even his closest group of friends, understands what his job is. My friends too, have no idea when it comes to what I do. As Rachel Green suggests of Chandler, I could be a '*transponster*'.

But all jokes aside, the widespread misunderstanding could be one of the biggest challenges to the role of the learning technologist in educational institutions across the globe. What is it that we do? "*It's technology right? That means printers? Hardware support? Oh, can you upload my presentations to Blackboard?*".

Wrong.

The 'Learning Technologist' has two words in the title, but for some reason the latter one is often emphasised. In reality, the Learning Technologist is a complex professional (and academic) role, and its variations and derivatives have increased over the years. This diversification of the role could be related to the maturity of educational technology and what we need to support our specific implementations, or perhaps even as a result of the financial crisis and the casualisation of the workforce. Regardless of your utopian or dystopian viewpoints, the increasing variations are not helpful in defining what it is that we do and how colleagues may perceive us. Oliver suggests the practices of Learning Technologists are "*little understood, even within their own community*" (Oliver, 2010).

So, what is it?

If we begin by trying to generalise the role, which is always dangerous, we can then hopefully explore it from a useful starting position. Think of the Learning Technologist as the middle person in the complex relationship between learning and teaching, and technology. Typically, the role involves a good appreciation of both elements. Critically though, a thorough understanding of learning and teaching precludes an understanding of technology. This is imperative, as we must first identify the challenges, within and of, pedagogy, before applying theory to practice. If we don't understand these core aspects of what it is to learn, or indeed to teach, how can we possibly advise on how technology might be an influencing and enhancing intervention? The understanding of technology and its place in education, for me at least, will always come second. Thus the role of the Learning Technologist sits comfortably alongside academic staff within curriculum development initiatives with a particular focus on applying theory to practice.

I also like to view the role of the Learning Technologist on a sliding continuum or spectrum amongst its variations. Learning Technologists often are the people responsible for managing the Virtual Learning Environment (VLE) in many institutions, dealing with the support and troubleshooting on a daily basis. Keeping with the Harry Potter reference earlier, the VLE is invariably the wand that us magicians keep so very close. It's not uncommon for people in these roles to rarely be involved in curriculum development alongside course teams. They might however be more involved with system architecture - more akin to an IT Services department. On the other end of the spectrum, you might also see people with little understanding of technology, but a more thorough understanding of education and educational development. Does that make either group any less of a Learning Technologist? No, because over the years the variation from one role to the next has shifted how we come to think of the role and indeed, how it is perceived. Furthermore, the range of technologies available, and the roles and tasks required to support their implementation, demand a variation of the role.

Historically, the role has also seen confusion with research. As far back as 2004, Conole has argued that such a wide variation in the Learning Technologist has been "*a strength in terms of the range of expertise but is also a weakness in terms of a lack of common shared understanding*" (Conole, 2004). Shurville et al. (2009) also emphasise the diversity in such roles. Let us now unpick this misunderstanding further (see Figure 1).

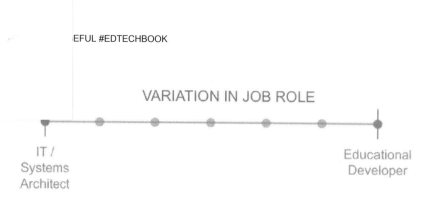

Figure 1. Variation in Job Role

VARIATIONS IN LEARNING TECHNOLOGY SUPPORT

The Association for Learning Technology (ALT) in the United Kingdom suggests Learning Technologists are "*people who are actively involved in managing, researching, supporting or enabling learning with the use of learning technology*" (ALT, 2013). This is a friendly and succinct framing of the role, however it's also quite broad and the lived reality is often something messier.

Typically Learning Technologists will be working on very different things from one institution to the next, and indeed, potentially even within the same institution. My own lived examples have seen this in action. However, as Learning Technologists have become embedded within the fabric of the university and a focal point of the student experience, what is needed to plug a gap in one institution can be as unique as that institution and its very students. To this end, there are three inextricably intertwined concepts impacting on how we perceive the role of the Learning Technologist: variations in job title, variations in their location, and the technical management of learning technologies.

- *Variation in job title*

In response to one of my blog posts on the subject, Phil Vincent (Technology Enhanced Learning Manager, York St. John University) made a pertinent comment - he identified the range of vacant Learning Technologist variants that were recruiting at the time across the UK: Learning Technologist; Education Advisor (Technology Enhanced Learning); Academic Technologist; eLearning Coordinator/Officer/Advisor/Consultant. The list goes on, and increasingly is prefixed or suffixed with 'assistant' or 'senior'. Personally, I've held positions of

'Learning Technology Development Officer' (although did extremely little 'development'), 'Lecturer & eLearning Coordinator', and my current role, 'Lecturer (Learning Technology)'.

What is very noticeable amongst these variations is not only fluctuation of the expectations and requirements for the role, but also in the salary. Salary is a particularly difficult thing to address within the role of the Learning Technologist as institutions pay differently all across the country, London weighting aside. A post-92 institution may pay significantly less than a Russell Group University, for a role that in practice is reasonably similar.

Added to this mix is the variation in title - do established learning technology teams need someone to maintain and manage administrative systems or process basic content development tasks, or do they require engagement at an academic level - someone who will teach, demonstrate good practice in Technology Enhanced Learning and furthermore, communicate with academic staff at that level? These are factors that can influence the role and the salary, but it is increasingly confusing when the same job title is applied to roles on opposite ends of the spectrum.

Whilst Conole (2004) reflected on a shift from multi-functional 'first-generation' Learning Technologists to a 'second-generation' who 'specialise' (in research), it might be logical to conclude the current state of wide variation is a potential third-generation Learning Technologist - somewhat different to its predecessors and who have found their place more from institutional direction, and undoubtedly a result of financial pressures, opposed to a personal preference. Shurville et al. (2009) suggest a need for professional bodies and documentation of practice for wider recognition of status, which could be one way to bring together and make sense of the variations. Obvious opportunities in the UK lie in ALT's Certified Membership scheme (CMALT) or through Fellowship to the Higher Education Academy (FHEA), but to what degree are these opportunities restricted to a certain type of role? Could all of the variations of the Learning Technologist discussed suitably demonstrate their suitability?

- *Variation in Location*

The breadth of titles and roles that commonly fall under the umbrella 'Learning Technologist' term are often a result of strategic thinking and planning. Quite who is doing this strategic thinking and planning however, adds a further dimension to the already complex discussion that is unfolding.

Learning technology teams are typically considered a professional service - some institutions, (which Selwyn suggests is derogatory) consider them 'non-academic', non-Faculty' or 'support' staff (Selwyn, 2014, p56), but the very placement of the team can have consequences for the role and how they are seen by academic staff: "*Given that structural location may significantly determine the influences a field is both exposed to and identified with (and thus what becomes valued), such structural decisions may have profound effects on the nature of the field in certain settings*" (Czerniewicz, 2008 p.176).

So what then, are the implications for learning technology teams when based within a library service? Or an IT department? How does this differ from one based within a Centre for Learning & Teaching, or further still, from specific roles based within Faculty? As Czerniewicz suggests, this placement can impact on the focus and direction for a team, as well as how they're perceived by academic staff. What follows attempts to provide a flavour in the variation in TEL provision and support in some UK HEIs.

In her blog post, Amber Thomas (Service Owner: Academic Technology at the University of Warwick) shares her experience from being based in an IT department and questions whether or not she's a Learning Technologist (Thomas, 2014). Amber's key interests lie in: "*the place of digital technology in the student experience; solutions development and architectures that support the workflows of academics and students; the way that organisational cultures and individuals' practices change; and what the web means to the creation and sharing of knowledge*". Sounds good right? This is a perfect example of the range of roles and without a doubt, her own role and that of her team is indispensable to the setup they have at the University of Warwick. It does not make her and her team any less of a 'Learning Technologist', but it does emphasise the increasing complexities of supporting learning technologies across universities.

At Leeds Beckett University the eLearning Strategy is developed and coordinated through the Centre for Learning & Teaching (CLT) by the Head of eLearning. This is an academic post with a remit to strategically engage academic staff in the use of digital tools and technology as an integrated part of their curriculum design. This role is supported by Faculty Learning Technologists who work locally with Associated Deans for Student Experience to implement change at a grass roots level. CLT works closely with the Learning Systems team who are a Library service and they "own" and provide technical support and development for all of the University's learning systems (VLE, Lecture Capture etc). In terms of staff development CLT, Learning Systems Team and Learning Technologists often run joint development sessions, each with a distinct development role and function. The Learning Systems team generally provide training on tools and functionality within a system, the Centre for Learning & Teaching then run sessions and activities around appropriate and effective use of these tools for learning & teaching, whilst the Learning Technologists provide support with regards to local course team use of the technologies within specific subject areas.

In my own experience, other institutions have different approaches to the support of Technology Enhanced Learning. Consider the approach at one of my old haunts, Edge Hill University, for whom, like many, Technology Enhanced Learning support was spurred along with the funded Centre for Excellence in Teaching and Learning in the early 2000's. Their close relationship between the SOLSTICE CETL and the Learning Technology Development (LTD) Team adopted a Hub and Spoke approach to Technology Enhanced Learning in an attempt to provide a central university service whilst achieving impact within faculties. The LTD team is based within the Library Service and carries a broad remit, administering and managing the VLE and other key tools, as well as engaging with curriculum development across the institution. Further, the CETL funded a number of 'SOLSTICE Fellows' dispersed across Faculties and Schools. Their remit was to not only engage in scholarship and research activity around Technology Enhanced Learning, but to also act as a key contact for academic colleagues. Over time this role developed to the funding of a 'Senior SOLSTICE Fellow' within each Faculty who might impact on and champion local strategic implementation of Technology Enhanced Learning.

At Manchester Metropolitan University, Neil Ringan heads up a diverse 'Learning Innovation' team - comprising a 'Classroom Technology Advisor', a number of 'Technology Enhanced Learning Advisors' (TELA) and 'Senior Lecturers in Learning Technologies'. The TELA roles, although funded centrally, are physically located within faculty - a direct attempt to become embedded in core processes.

My current role as a 'Lecturer (Learning Technology)' is based in (and funded by) the Faculty of Health and Life Sciences at the University of Liverpool. My role sits at the centre of the Faculty within the Institute of Learning and Teaching, with identical roles based within each of the six schools of the Faculty. These academic roles have been introduced within the Faculty to drive high level thinking in Technology Enhanced Learning and are complemented by a support team comprising 'TEL Technicians'. This Faculty approach runs in conjunction with the central 'eLearning Unit' (eLU) based within the Centre for Lifelong Learning. eLU consists of a number of learning technologist who engage in various tasks such as supporting staff in using the VLE, curriculum development, teaching on the University L&T qualifications, and staff development, etc.

These setups each have their pros and cons. It's not uncommon for central based roles to have the keys to the kingdom - full admin access to systems to research and configure. Often faculty-based roles do not have this level of access, but can have the benefit of being embedded within the core processes of the Faculty - something that is a recurring challenge in TEL provision. The 'correct' approach to Technology Enhanced Learning support may never be realised however, because every institution is different. The success of implementing TEL is not just reliant upon a strategy (however good it might be), but ultimately upon the people on the ground employed to implement it. This applies from the top down - the senior colleagues driving strategy and breaking down barriers; through to academic staff willing to step out of their comfort zones; and those roles working to support and encourage them to do so. A good strategy without the people will never succeed. The right people, regardless of strategy, will always innovate and question the status quo. Finding a balance that fits the institution, the staff and the students…

well that can be the basis for something great! Whether that is based on a central team approach, a dispersed-but-centrally-coordinated team, or even local Faculty approaches, learning technology support and provision should be agile, proactive and responsive.

- *Technical Management of Learning Technologies*

The responsibilities for management of learning technologies have obvious implications for the roles required to support them. If a University decides to outsource the hosting of the VLE they might choose to focus their Learning Technologist on supporting its implementation. However if they decide to host these services internally a significant resource is logically directed to technical management and maintenance. Again neither approach is 'the right way' - there might be a 'bit of both' in some institutions and of course, there are pros and cons to each. However, these are critical decisions that influence an institution's support for Technology Enhanced Learning and are reflected in the roles and tasks employed to do so. At the University of Liverpool, the Blackboard VLE is hosted internally and managed by the 'Technology Enhanced Learning and Research' team within the central Computer Services Department. This team might work on integrations with University systems and manage back-end processes with Blackboard, and work in conjunction with the eLearning Unit. Edge Hill University has gone for the Blackboard managed hosting service and MMU call on the services of ULCC to host their Moodle platform. Once again, there are pros and cons and both approaches require significant investment to provide a robust service.

SUMMARY

So what is a Learning Technologist? Well, it depends. As has been demonstrated throughout this chapter, the role of the Learning Technologist can include a subtle underpinning of learning and teaching, and technology. Perhaps even research. Depending on the unique approach at any institution the role might contain a greater or lesser emphasis to either, but any pattern, such as the shift identified by Conole, is difficult to visualise now. Furthermore, the placement of the Learning Technologist within a complex organisational structure adds greater variation to the roles required to support Technology Enhanced Learning within any institution. As the expectations upon technology as the panacea to improve student [insert one of: retention / attainment / flexibility / satisfaction] increase, so to will the variation of roles employed to support their implementation. Quite 'what a Learning Technologist is' may not be definitively concluded in the near future, but a demand for these roles will inevitably continue to soar as institutions grapple to introduce technology as a key factor in supporting learning, teaching and assessment. As we move to a post-digital era, and with continued financial pressures on institutions, the variations of the Learning Technologist discussed in this chapter will not cease any time soon.

ACKNOWLEDGEMENTS

Special thanks go to those who supported the development and accuracy of the information in this chapter, including:

Simon Thompson, Head of eLearning at Leeds Beckett University

Neil Ringan, Head of Learning Innovation at Manchester Metropolitan University

Megan Juss, Learning Technology Development Manager at Edge Hill University.

It would also be remiss to exclude David Hopkins, Phil Vincent, Sheila McNeill and Amber Thomas (as well as the entire ALT-Members email list) for ongoing discussion and debate in the area of 'What is a Learning Technologist').

REFERENCES

Association for Learning Technology (ALT). (2014). *What is Learning Technology?*. Oxford, England: Association for Learning Technology. Available at: http://www.alt.ac.uk/about-alt/what-learning-technology [Accessed 26.8.2014].

Conole, G. (2004). "The Role Of Learning Technology Practitioners And Researchers In Understanding Networked Learning". In: Proceedings of the Third International Conference on Networked Learning 2004. Lancaster University, England, UK, 5-7 April 2004. Available at: http://www.networkedlearningconference.org.uk/past/nlc2004/proceedings/symposia/symposium1/conole.htm [Accessed 23.11.2013].

Czerniewicz, L. (2008). "Distinguishing the Field of Educational Technology". The Electronic Journal of e-Learning, 6(3), pp. 171-178. Available at: http://www.ejel.org/volume6/issue3/p171 [Accessed 23.10.2013].

Oliver, M. (2002) "What do Learning Technologists do?". Innovations in Education and Teaching International, 39(4), pp. 245-252. Available at: http://dx.doi.org/10.1080/13558000210161089 [Accessed 21.10.2013].

Selwyn, N (2014) Digital Technology and the Contemporary University: Degrees of digitazation. Routledge.

Shurville, S., Browne, T. & Whitaker, M. (2009). "Accommodating the newfound strategic importance of educational technologists within higher education. A critical literature review". Campus-Wide Information Systems, 26(3), pp. 201-231. Available at: http://dx.doi.org/10.1108/10650740910967384 [Accessed 7.8.2014].

Thomas, A (2014) Perhaps I'm Not One? Amber at Warwick: Academic Technology. http://amberatwarwick.wordpress.com/2014/11/10/perhaps-im-not-one/ [Accessed 11.11.14]

CITATION

Reed, P. (2015). The structure and roles of Learning Technologists within Higher Education Institutions. In: Hopkins, D., ed., *The Really Useful #EdTechBook*, 1st ed. David Hopkins, pp.41-51.

LEARNING TECHNOLOGISTS AS AGENTS OF CHANGE: BLENDING POLICY AND CREATIVITY

RACHEL CHALLEN

eLearning Manager, Loughborough College

@RKChallen

http://blogs.loucoll.ac.uk/learningtechnology/

Rachel is the eLearning Manager at Loughborough College; passionate about education technology and the positive impact it can have, directly and indirectly, on the student experience. Current work streams include operational responsibility for embedding the recommendations of FELTAG within the College and exploring the opportunities provided by technology for widening and enhancing participation in education. Rachel is currently undertaking a Doctorate in Education focusing on online pedagogy and digital skills.

"The success of any kind of social epidemic is heavily dependent on the involvement of people with a particular and rare set of social gifts." (Gladwell, 2002 pg 33)

Welcome! Its very nice to see you and have your company for the next few pages in this wonderful book and share my reflections of 12 years experience as a Learning Technologist in a private ePortfolio company, Higher Education and Further Education. This chapter will show how I believe that, as a group, our professional characteristics cover the 3 main skill sets of Connector, Maven, and Salesperson that Gladwell (2002) describes as inherent to a set of people that are influential and that are a mode of transmission for supporting change and institutional strategic goals.

When I first thought about what I wanted to cover in this chapter my overriding feeling was that, as a group of people, Learning Technologists make things happen and present often mystical (to the audience) solutions which led to my feeling of 'magic'. As I was thinking through the structure of the chapter though, my mind kept skipping between magicians and agents of change. When I look back at the titles, I think they are more or less the same; making something happen that may not be an obvious outcome, something that may needs abstract thinking, something that needs the full involvement and buy in of the audience connecting them together in a joint experience and something that makes you think 'wow'.

Learning technology, as a social epidemic (Gladwell, 2002), requires a group of people who can 'tip' people into change, a group of people who are well connected within their institution, and externally (but that's a different discussion), and a group of people who can make change 'sticky' by adapting and selling one message to different groups. It is this more than anything that I think sets Learning Technologists apart. The ability to talk many different [pedagogical] languages and solve problems has a strong correlation with another agent, not of change but a secret one – Danger Mouse (did you know he can talk 34 different languages including alien). Bear with me, yes, it probably is a bit strange that a super hero is here, in this chapter, but in my opinion there are many shared aspects between Learning Technologists and superheroes (you heard it here first!) purely because of the things we are asked to do, the outcomes we have to achieve and the characteristics we share:

- **Persistence** - It's very rare that superheroes or Learning Technologists will be defeated, there is always a plan B
- **Reactive** - Ready to spring into action at any point and being able to defeat the 'baddies' when they surprise you (network and system issues)
- **Motivation or a sense of responsibility** - We want staff to engage and students to benefit, our work is focused on removing barriers and making this happen
- **A supporting cast** – The learning technology community is always there to

help out in times of strife

- **Psychokinetic** - And probably the most important characteristic; the ability to make 'broken' technology work just by standing next to someone's desk!

So for me, being a Learning Technologist is less about specific skills, even within this book the actual skill sets vary greatly by author, and more about the characteristics of connectors and influencers sprinkled with a liberal dose of patience and a touch of superhero.

So how can the characteristics of Learning Technologists create pathways of change between the needs of policy, strategy, teaching and learning and the needs of specific student groups? As a group of professionals, we are ideally placed to be part of change and development conversations in most departments; teaching, learning, assessment, systems and registry, to name but a few. Due to this connector role, we hold the key to be able to facilitate step changes and impact positively on existing paradigms.

Of course, most decisions are made for institutional strategic purposes and it is vital that executive direction is transparent. Julian Stodd (2014a) puts forward that for the process of change to become sticky, it needs to be co-owned and co-created by the community:

> *"change is not one story that you write that gets cascaded down through the structure. Rather, the story is co-created at each level throughout the organisation, made relevant to each group in each retelling. Or at least it is if you want it to stick. This does, of course, mean that your story can evolve, but that's really the whole point of it: it will evolve to be more relevant to each group that hears it. Good change projects engage people at every level, supporting them in creating a new meaning in the moment and sharing that through narratives."* (Figure 1)

Figure 1: Organisation and change (Stodd, 2014b)

This process of enabling change is one of the most immeasurable impacts of a Learning Technologist because it goes beyond analytics and tick-boxes; it's about building confidence, passion and allowing those new stories and meanings to evolve. System change in particular can elicit a strong emotional response as staff have invested time using the systems and they have a sense of ownership and feel part of a 'tribe', and the loss of this through a changing of systems can have a very detrimental effect on how effective the change process is. The loyalty to a system can be seen as an extension or an external indicator of a persons identity which matches with others in a community or, as Hughes (2000, pg.21) explains it, a tribal group that develops "*its own culture, heroes, hierarchy, language*" with a fierce loyalty towards each other. This has to be taken into account, even with a small step change, as these 'tribes' become the influencers and have the power to steer the success of any project that requires buy-in. Take a system based project for changing a VLE as an example; it is essential that the staff and students are involved and are allowed to steer and own these decisions. Learning Technologists are key to this as we are the conduit between teachers and system – we understand what the teacher wants and can translate that into system functionality requirements. We can help open channels of communications and add depth to the rich storytelling of needs as knowledge and an understanding of the issues as they grow. As long as there is a clear outcome, however large or small, this inclusive and consultative process gives value to stakeholders and will positively impact on the success of change.

Opening those lines of communication also means that, along with the really positive and exciting ideas, the barriers and challenges that people experience when using technology to support teaching and learning also have a space to be shared. What I've experienced is that those fears are generally the same "*What will happen if the technology breaks*", "*What will happen if the students know more than I do*", "*I don't want to be replaced by technology*" or even "*my students don't like technology*". I would be surprised if you haven't heard any of these before, and a lot more besides, and will have your own answers and strategies buried away to counteract them. For these occasions the importance of the Learning Technologist as a connector, influencer and storyteller becomes even more apparent. This is also when your superhero persistence will come in very useful!

So we've chatted about the change process that needs to happen when an institution is changing its internal cultural paradigm but what about when a policy is imposed from a higher realm? In Further Education (FE) this happens on a regular basis and hence there is a very reactive culture due to the nature of constantly shifting Governmental policies and funding decisions. As a whole, it is a very important sector which provides a range of access, levels, courses and pathways. This enables traditional and non-traditional learners to access education which may not have been previously available to them and develop the transferable skills that are needed for successful employment. However, until recently, digital skills haven't been consistently high on the agenda and although there is a myriad of legacy Technology Enhanced Learning (TEL) policies - the success and impact of these have been explored elsewhere in this book - the most recent report and current topic of discussion in the sector is the recommendations of the Further Education Learning Technology Action Group (FELTAG).

In March 2014, the FELTAG board made a number of recommendations to the Department of Business, Innovation and Skills (BIS) that were intended to support the use of digital resources in a sound, sustainable manner for the benefit of widening learning opportunities and developing digital literacy for staff and students. The recommendations also included the edict of developing a certain percentage (initially 10%) of each programme in the existing curriculum to online learning. It is very clear that for this initiative to be successful there needs to be a tangible culture change that embeds the use of TEL as part of the teaching toolkit, ensuring it has real learner impact with a clear link to learning outcomes.

BIS subsequently published a response to FELTAG in June 2014 and broadly accepted the recommendations with the addition of linking the online learning percentage to an online funding rate. Eight months later, there is still a lack of real clarification regarding funding, online learning definitions and timelines, however Learning Technologists in FE are trying to make sense of the way forward. Not to just tick the funding box, but to build plans of action that will make a real difference for staff, students and the institution for the long term. This is evident with the sheer amount of conversations that FELTAG has instigated through external formal and informal networks, resulting in those networks co-creating stories that will input into the change process. In my institution this is also happening internally through meetings, presentations and technology celebration days (eLearning Team, 2014) but the results from a national temperature check survey facilitated by Charlie Williams (2014), shows an alarming lack of institutional awareness towards FELTAG. In fact, even though it was a fairly small sample of 71 responses, it showed that although most respondees have heard about FELTAG this has mostly happened from sources outside of the institution. This is an indication that the cultural shift needed to successfully implement FELTAG within institutions isn't happening across the whole sector, and that those conversations must urgently start to enable the series of small step changes that are needed. Learning Technologists are ideally placed to support this transformational development with the support of the institution.

A key consideration when working with teachers to implement FELTAG is how to change expectations of successful curriculum design for online learning. A teacher would not walk into a classroom, put a whole bunch of documents on the table with little or no explanation and expect 100% engagement and achievement; and yet when this happens in the VLE, it is often considered online learning with the technology getting the blame if achievement isn't on target. The SAMR model (Puentedura, 2014) takes the development and use of technology in teaching and learning from substitution to redefinition. Doing what we've always done but online (substitution) is not going to achieve a long term culture change, but thinking about how technology can bring a new dimension (redefinition) has a much higher chance of online learning being embedded in a meaningful and intended way. This process isn't easy and does require for some, an almost seismic shift in thinking. It is down to Learning Technologists as agents of change to support, facilitate and 'tip' our teaching communities into thinking holistically about Technology Enhanced Learning and how it can have a massive positive impact on teaching and learning.

So there we have it. Learning Technologists as agents of change and general superheroes – battling against pedagogy crime and sweeping the country with a social epidemic of online learning …. I'm off to get my cape.

REFERENCES

Department for Business, Innovation and Skills, (2014). Government Response to the recommendations from the Further Education Learning Technology Action Group (FELTAG).

FELTAG: Paths forward to a digital future for Further Education and Skills. (2014). [online] Further Education Learning Technology Action Group. Available at: http://feltag.org.uk/wp-content/uploads/2012/01/FELTAG-REPORT-FINAL.pdf [Accessed 27 Mar. 2014].

Gladwell, M. (2002). Tipping point. Jakarta: Gramedia Pustaka Utama.

Hughes, B. (2000). Dust or magic. Harlow, England: Addison-Wesley.

Puentedura, R. (2014). SAMR. [Blog] Ruben R. Puentedura's Weblog. Available at: http://www.hippasus.com/rrpweblog/ [Accessed 14 Nov. 2014].

eLearning Team. (2014). Roll up Roll up - Loughborough College Technology Celebration Day - what was it all about?. [Blog] Blog and Information from the eLearning Team at Loughborough College. Available at: http://blogs.loucoll.ac.uk/learningtechnology/2014/10/23/looking-back-on-technology-celebration-day/ [Accessed 23 Oct. 2014].

Stodd, J. (2014a). The co-ownership of #change. [Blog] Julian Stodd's Learning Blog. Available at:

http://julianstodd.wordpress.com/2013/10/08/the-co-ownership-of-change/ [Accessed 24 Nov. 2014].

Organisation and Change (2014b) [Illustration] Available at:
http://julianstodd.wordpress.com/2013/11/29/the-co-creation-and-co-ownership-of-organisational-change/
[Accessed 24th Nov. 2014].

Westera, W. (2004). On strategies of educational innovation: Between substitution and transformation.
Higher Education, 47(4), pp.501-517.

Williams, C. (2014). uk FeLearning FELTAG Survey. [Blog] uk FeLearning. Available at:
http://ukfelearning.blogspot.co.uk/ [Accessed 27 Nov. 2014].

CITATION

Challen, R. (2015). Learning Technologists as agents of change: blending policy and creativity. In: Hopkins, D., ed., *The Really Useful #EdTechBook*, 1st ed. David Hopkins, pp.53-60.

DEVELOPING THE SKILLS AND KNOWLEDGE OF A LEARNING TECHNOLOGIST

JULIE WEDGWOOD

@juliewedgwood

http://www.juliewedgwood.com

Julie has worked across a wide range of industry sectors in the UK, EMEA and USA over the last 25 years, gaining recognition as a leading learning architect, a thought leader in blended learning design, and an active curator and exponent of learning technology, which led to her being described as the trainer's trainer. Julie is an accredited lecturer at Derby University, designs experiential learning, eLearning, learning games and simulation-based eLearning, and is currently writing a book about the practicalities of managing online learning communities.

INTRODUCTION

Over the last 15 years the eruption of learning technology and digital tools has led to the emergence of the role of Learning Technologist, and with it, a series of defacto learning technology tools, standards and new learning strategies have materialized, creating a wave of new ideas, approaches and methods that are re-writing the pedagogical and andragogical models of the past.

Whether you are a seasoned professional or new to education or the Learning and Development sector, understanding the tools and technologies that are now tried, trusted and in effect, seen as essential by many Learning Technologists have to be worth exploring. However, "*Where do I start?*" is a familiar reaction heard from many who need to catch up with the changes and who may be feeling a little overwhelmed by the continual developments appearing within the sector.

This lament is often used as a barrier to engagement, and my answer is always the same: Start anywhere! If a particular learning technology tool or strategy interests you, and you think you might be able to harness it in your teaching practice, that's a great place to start.

I have found that many in education (either academic or corporate) who say that they don't understand or use learning technology, often don't realize that they have already developed useful technologist skills as a natural part of living in the 21 century. The Learning Technology Skills & Knowledge Assessment below can be used to help teachers/trainers/L&D professionals to identify, and value, their level of knowledge and skills with learning technology. If approached with honesty, it will help identify those areas or aspects where perhaps it might be useful to expand knowledge and skills in more depth or into new areas.

What's your level of skill and knowledge?

LEARNING TECHNOLOGY SKILLS & KNOWLEDGE ASSESSMENT

The knowledge and skills of a Learning Technologist have been subdivided into fourteen categories and are represented by six statements. Consider each statement in turn. Then, using the scale below, rate how closely each statement matches to you right now and write that number on the line next to the statement. Finally total each category set.

Scale: **1** That's not me. **2** To some degree that's me. **3** That's pretty much like me. **4** That's definitely me.

ACCESSIBILITY	
I know that learning materials should be adaptable for those with accessibility needs.	
I use and recommend accessibility features in Adobe Acrobat Reader, embed audio in documents, and use screen reader friendly fonts and font sizes.	
I use and promote the adoption of accessible fonts, font sizes, colour, layout use in learning materials.	
I know and promote the accessible features of popular software.	
I know how to adapt a presentation to be suitable for learners with visual/auditory impairment.	
I have a qualification in accessible IT practice.	
ACCESSIBILITY TOTAL:	

Scale: **1** That's not me. **2** To some degree that's me. **3** That's pretty much like me. **4** That's definitely me.

VIDEO	
I use/incorporate video into learning delivery.	
I make videos using my phone or a digital camera/video camera.	
I understand the different formats and quality of video files.	
I can edit video to an acceptable standard.	
I have a You Tube or similar channel, that I publish videos on for use by my organisation or the public.	
I write, direct and produce video for learning.	
VIDEO TOTAL:	

Scale: **1** That's not me. **2** To some degree that's me. **3** That's pretty much like me. **4** That's definitely me.

GRAPHIC DESIGN	
I use a variety of different sources to find appropriate graphics to support my learning designs.	
I specify the requirements for a graphic designer to develop the graphics to support learning.	
I design my own graphics.	
I apply the principles of usability.	
I am aware of the principles of graphic design.	
I am aware of the principles of heuristics.	
GRAPHIC DESIGN TOTAL:	

Scale: **1** That's not me. **2** To some degree that's me. **3** That's pretty much like me. **4** That's definitely me.

SYNCHRONOUS ENVIRONMENTS	
I attend online synchronous events.	
I administer online synchronous events.	
I teach/present in synchronous environments.	
I can manage text and audio discussions in synchronous events effectively.	
I can managing online synchronous breakout groups.	
I have a qualification in the delivery of online synchronous events. (Eg COLF).	
SYNCHRONOUS ENVIRONMENTS TOTAL:	

Scale: **1** That's not me. **2** To some degree that's me. **3** That's pretty much like me. **4** That's definitely me.

DIGITAL LITERACY	
I use the Internet .	
I am comfortable using word processors, spreadsheets, search engines.	
I use online security tools.	
I use presentation software.	
I create PDFs.	
I use blogging/microblogging software (such as WordPress, Twitter, Facebook).	
DIGITAL LITERACY TOTAL:	

Scale: **1** That's not me. **2** To some degree that's me. **3** That's pretty much like me. **4** That's definitely me.

CURATION	
I understand the concepts of curation for learning.	
I use RSS or other methods to automatically identify new information related to my interests.	
I curate content for myself.	
I curate content for others.	
I review and analyse the curation of others to identify trends relevant to my sector.	
I define and implement curation strategies.	
CURATION TOTAL:	

Scale: 1 That's not me. **2** To some degree that's me. **3** That's pretty much like me. **4** That's definitely me.

MOBILE	
I use a smartphone/tablet/phablet.	
I understand the benefits of mobile learning.	
I communicate using a variety of Apps on my smartphone/tablet/phablet.	
I use photo/video editing and sharing Apps.	
I regularly find Apps that are relevant to learning, communication, my sector.	
I have successfully implemented mobile learning solutions.	
MOBILE TOTAL:	

Scale: 1 That's not me. **2** To some degree that's me. **3** That's pretty much like me. **4** That's definitely me.

AUDIO	
I use music as part of learning.	
I download and listen to podcasts.	
I understand the copyright laws for music and audio materials and how they relate to my role/organization.	
I can embed audio files into standard software such as word processors/spreadsheets/presentation software.	
I edit audio files using an editor such as Audacity.	
I create and publish podcasts either internally within my company or with an external organization.	
AUDIO TOTAL:	

Scale: 1 That's not me. **2** To some degree that's me. **3** That's pretty much like me. **4** That's definitely me.

SHARING / COLLABORATING	
I use at least one shared workspace eg Dropbox/SharePoint/Cloud services.	
I present my learning developments/theories with others at conferences or collaborative groups related to my sector.	
I use wikis/discussion boards/internal social media channels as part of my job role.	
I regularly share thoughts and information with others via social media or other channels (external to my organisation).	
I write a blog on a regular basis	
I design shared workspaces and/or collaborative environments.	
SHARING / COLLABORATION TOTAL:	

Scale: 1 That's not me. **2** To some degree that's me. **3** That's pretty much like me. **4** That's definitely me.

DESIGNING / CREATING	
I design learning.	
I am familiar with the principles of instructional design.	
I use one or more eLearning authoring tools.	
I have a qualification in instructional design/5+years experience as an instructional designer.	
I regularly review learning design developments and new strategies.	
I use a variety of different design strategies depending on the learning requirements.	
DESIGNING / CREATING TOTAL:	

Scale: 1 That's not me. **2** To some degree that's me. **3** That's pretty much like me. **4** That's definitely me.

GAMIFICATION / GAMES FOR LEARNING	
I play digital games for work and/or leisure.	
I understand the benefits of gamification for learning.	
I am familiar with/use simulation environments.	
I am familiar with/use serious games.	
I am actively using gamification/games in learning delivery.	
I design learning that is gamified/uses games, simulations, simulated environments.	
GAMIFICATION / GAMES FOR LEARNING TOTAL:	

Scale: 1 That's not me. **2** To some degree that's me. **3** That's pretty much like me. **4** That's definitely me.

PERFORMANCE SUPPORT / EVALUATION	
I understand the difference between objectives and outcomes.	
I am familiar with the popular performance support theories.	
I include performance support in the design of learning.	
I am aware of different ways to measure the effectiveness of learning delivery.	
I use appropriate methods to test the effectiveness of learning delivery.	
I use a range of different media as performance support tools to address just in time/in case scenarios.	
PERFORMANCE SUPPORT / EVALUATION TOTAL:	

Scale: 1 That's not me. **2** To some degree that's me. **3** That's pretty much like me. **4** That's definitely me.

LEARNING MANAGEMENT	
I understand the concept of a Learning Management Systems (LMS).	
I can extract reports from the LMS in use at my job/organization.	
I understand the differences between Flash and HTML5, and what can be captured for analysis.	
I can use SCORM and other methods of linking content to an LMS.	
I can interpret learning management reports to identify the business/organisational centric information.	
I analyse learning management reports for trends and issues that need to be addressed to improve performance, and take appropriate action.	
LEARNING MANAGEMENT TOTAL:	

Scale: 1 That's not me. **2** To some degree that's me. **3** That's pretty much like me. **4** That's definitely me.

CONTINUOUS PROFESSIONAL DEVELOPMENT	
I track and report events I attend related to my professional development.	
I attend at least two national conferences per year to help me stay on top of the latest changes.	
I am an active member of group and/or association related to learning and development.	
I attend webinars and other events throughout the year related to education/teaching/training/my job/sector focus.	
I am a member of social networks related to my job/sector focus.	
I invest time in keeping up to date with developments in learning and the emerging approaches and strategies as they are adopted in my industry sector.	
CONTINUOUS PROFESSIONAL DEVELOPMENT TOTAL:	

RESULTS

For each category, enter your score, or shade in the box in the row that corresponds with the range where your score fails. For example if you scored 17 in Curation, you would shade in the middle box in that row; if you scored 13 in Video you would shade the right hand box in that row. When you have completed each row you will see a map of your range of learning technology knowledge and skills at a glance.

A score of 20-24 indicates a high level of knowledge/skill in that category of learning technology; 14-19 a moderate level and below 14 an underdeveloped level of knowledge/skill:

CATEGORY	SCORE 20-24 (HIGHLY DEVELOPED)	SCORE 14-19 (MODERATELY DEVELOPED)	SCORE BELOW 14 (UNDER DEVELOPED)
ACCESSIBILITY			
VIDEO			
GRAPHIC DESIGN			
SYNCHRONOUS ENVIRONMENTS			
DIGITAL LITERACY			
CURATION			
MOBILE			
AUDIO			
SHARING / COLLABORATING			
DESIGNING / CREATING			
GAMIFICATION / GAMES FOR LEARNING			
PERFORMANCE SUPPORT			
LEARNING MANAGEMENT			
CONTINUOUS PROFESSIONAL DEVELOPMENT			

HOW TO USE YOUR RESULTS

Hopefully by completing this assessment you have a clearer picture of where your current knowledge and skills with learning technology lie. Use this awareness to further develop your knowledge and skills with the learning technology available in the categories where you are underdeveloped or moderately underdeveloped and which relate to your situation.

On the following pages you will find a series of curated resources organized according to the assessment categories. Some of these resources might help you develop your skills, or might act as a handy go to reference. (Please Note: If you choose to use these resources, you use them at your own risk. It is your responsibility to protect yourself with relevant digital security measures.)

The list of resources is not an exhaustive list, just a starting point. These are resources that have proved useful to me and to my students both in higher education and corporate settings.

If you wouldd rather not copy out the links from the Reference pages (who would?), take a look at the Symbaloo webmixes I've created that contain all of the links listed to make it really easy for you to explore the online resources and retain those you find useful.

You will need to create a free account with Symbaloo if you do not already have one.

CREATING A SYMBALOO ACCOUNT

1. Open your preferred web browser and navigate to http://www.symbaloo.com.

2. Click *Login*.

3. Complete the account registration using either your *Facebook* or *Google* account or by *completing the form provided*. Accept the *terms and conditions* (after reading them of course!) and click *Create My Account*.

4. The Symbaloo Team will send you an email. Open the email to *verify your account*.

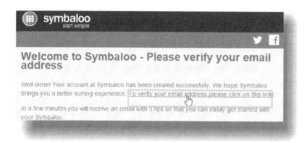

ACCESSING THE WEBMIXES

1. On the Symbaloo Menu bar, click on the *Tiles* drop down to change the search criteria to *Webmixes*.

2. In the Search box enter *#EdTechBook*. The five Webmixes will appear.

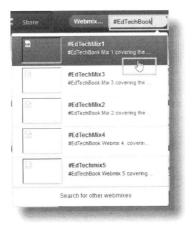

3. *Select* the Webmix you want to review.

4. The WebMix details and an image of the Webmix are shown. Click Add this *Webmix* to add the webmix to your account as a *Tab* at the top of the Symbaloo screen.

5. Repeat steps 2-4 as required.

Once one or more of the WebMixes are added to your account you can use them to explore the resources listed, simply click on the *Webmix Tab* and then on individual *Tiles*.

If you already have a Symbaloo account the following links might also be useful to you to go directly to a particular Webmix:

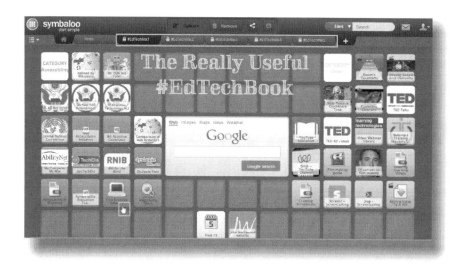

WEBMIX	CATEGORIES COVERED	LINK
#EdTechMix1	• Accessibility • Video • *(Find 15)*	http://www.symbaloo.com/mix/edtechmix11
#EdTechMix2	• Graphic Design • Synchronous Environments • Digital Literacy	http://www.symbaloo.com/mix/edtechmix2
#EdTechMix3	• Curation • Mobile • Audio	http://www.symbaloo.com/mix/edtechmix3
#EdTechMix4	• Sharing/Collaborating • Designing	http://www.symbaloo.com/mix/edtechmix4
#EdTechMix5	• Gamification / Games for Learning • Performance Support • Learning Management • Continuous Professional Development	http://www.symbaloo.com/mix/edtechmix5

'FIND 15' TO FIND THE TIME TO EXPLORE THE RESOURCES

If you look at the next few pages and consider what is listed to be a bit overwhelming, try my 'Find 15' minutes strategy for finding time for learning in a time hungry world. You'll find the link to it on *#EdTechMix1*.

ACCESSIBILITY RESOURCES

As a Learning Technologist it is important to understand the requirements for accessibility and design learning solutions that can be easily adapted to the particular needs of any learner with accessibility needs. However, it never ceases to amaze me how so many "accessibility tools" are actually really helpful to everyone, and I recommend taking a good look at what's out there (many tools are free) and seeing what you can do to improve your own understanding. You'll find the resources in *#EdTechMix1*

Definitions and the Law

- From Wikipedia – a good roundup of Accessibility Note: Scroll down the webpage to find: Disability, information technology (IT) and telecommunications.
  http://en.wikipedia.org/wiki/Accessibility

- A UK advisory service on technologies for accessibility and inclusion for disabled staff and students. http://www.jisctechdis.ac.uk/

- The United Nations Convention on the Rights of Persons with Disabilities.
  http://www.un.org/disabilities/default.asp?navid=12&pid=150

- The UK Disability and Discrimination Act.
  http://en.wikipedia.org/wiki/Disability_Discrimination_Act_1995

- Americans with Disabilities Act of 1990.
  http://en.wikipedia.org/wiki/Americans_with_Disabilities_Act_of_1990

- The amendment to the Americans with Disability Act 1990.
  http://en.wikipedia.org/wiki/Section_508_Amendment_to_the_Rehabilitation_Act_of_1973

- The US Assistive Technology Act 1998.
  http://en.wikisource.org/wiki/Assistive_Technology_Act_of_1998

- The World Wide Web Consortium (WC3) Accessibility Guideline.
  http://www.w3.org/WAI/intro/wcag

- The World Wide Web Consortium (WC3)Web Accessibility Initiative. http://www.w3.org/WAI/

Useful Information sources and tools

- From Wikipedia – A comparison of Web browsers.
  http://en.wikipedia.org/wiki/Comparison_of_web_browsers#Accessibility_features

- AbilityNet's utility to help learners customize their computer to their specific needs.
  http://www.abilitynet.org.uk/advice-info/my-computer-my-way

- The Royal National Institute for the Blind website information on synthetic speech.
  http://www.rnib.org.uk/search/site/audio

- Dyslexie: A font to assist learners who have/may have dyslexia.
  http://www.dyslexiefont.com/en/dyslexia-font/

- Free Assistive software: A series of accessibility applications that are free or low cost to
  download and use. http://www.fx-software.co.uk/assistive.htm

- A free onscreen virtual magnifying glass for enlarging parts of the screen.
  http://sourceforge.net/projects/magnifier/ (This is also useful when presenting/teaching if fine
  detail is difficult for some in the class/audience to read.)

- Epicentre white paper on accessibility in e-learning. http://epicentre.co.uk/central/wp-
  content/uploads/2012/11/INS_accessibility_in_e-learning.pdf

- The World Wide Web Consortium (WC3) Web Accessibility Evaluation Tools List.
  http://www.w3.org/WAI/ER/tools/#General

VIDEO RESOUCES

In the media driven world, video is the new standard, and the ability to seamlessly integrate video into your learning delivery, be it video that you have produced, or content from the web, should be a skill that every teacher/trainer has, along with a solid understanding of the related copyright law. You Tube never ceases to amaze me as to what fantastic content can be found to support a wide variety of subjects, and I found that many of my students would far prefer to watch a video than read a chapter of a book, in order gain an understanding of an idea or concept. You'll find the resources in *#EdTechMix1*.

- Blooms Taxonomy explained using the film "Pirates of the Caribbean".
  https://www.youtube.com/watch?v=tNGFDENxL5U

1. Exploring diversity : Nick Vujicic's inspirational "No arms, no legs, no worries".

https://www.youtube.com/watch?v=Gc4HGQHgeFE

2. The value of good body posture and how it can affect your confidence: Amy Cuddy, tells her personal story. https://www.youtube.com/watch?v=Ks-_Mh1QhMc

3. Valuing people living with Dementia. https://www.youtube.com/watch?v=U08lAYIdZlE

4. It does take time to source and critically review suitable material to recommend to students/learners, so don't underestimate the time it can take to find quality solutions using YouTube or other online channels. A good place to start might be: The education videos YouTube channel. https://www.youtube.com/education

'How to' guides

- From Onlignment, a solid introduction to creating learning videos. http://onlignment.com/wp-content/uploads/2011/04/A-practical-guide-to-creating-learning-videos.pdf

- From Onlignment, a short guide to creating screencasts. http://onlignment.com/wp-content/uploads/2011/04/A-practical-guide-to-creating-learning-screencasts.pdf

- How to add video to PDF's. https://www.youtube.com/watch?v=4qxQ1UZbmxk

- Film making guide. http://www.thackraymedicalmuseum.co.uk/library-resources/collections-research/medicine-at-the-movies/ (Scroll down to access the link to Film Making Project – A short guide PDF).

- Mark Copeman's invaluable 10 secrets to successful video production in learning. https://www.timetag.tv/learningtechnologies/play/22946

Useful Websites and tools

- A YouTube channel devoted to sharing how to do lots of different things in no more than five minutes. https://www.youtube.com/user/5minStudio/videos

- Web based Screen recorder. https://www.screenr.com/

- Easy to use screen recorder/capture software. http://www.techsmith.com/jing.html

- Powtoon.com a simple animated presentation tool. http://www.powtoon.com/

- Ted Talks. http://www.ted.com/ If you've not come across these, be prepared to become an addict! Check out their Education specific Channel. http://www.ted.com/watch/ted-ed

- Recordings of the Trainingindustry.com's webinars. http://www.trainingindustry.com/webinars.aspx

- The Learning Technologies Conference sessions and webinars. https://www.timetag.tv/learningtechnologies

Book

Brindle M., *The Digital Filmmaking Handbook*, Quercus Editions Ltd, London, 2013

GRAPHIC DESIGN RESOURCES

As with video, good graphics that support the delivery of learning are a must in my view. From presentation slides, to infographics, diagrams and animations, it's important to understand how to construct graphics that will act as a good aid to learning. You'll find the resources in *#EdTechMix2*.

Graphic design core background information

- From Wikipedia: Usability engineering. http://en.wikipedia.org/wiki/Usability_engineering

- Jakob Neilson's 10 heuristics, which are widely quoted and used in usability evaluation. http://en.wikipedia.org/wiki/Heuristic_evaluation

- A course on Graphic Design from Lynda.com. http://www.lynda.com/Design-training-tutorials/40-0.html?utm_source=google&utm_medium=cpc&utm_campaign=Search-Dsg-Graphic+Design&utm_content=55860110586&utm_term=%2Blearning%20%2Bgraphic%20%2Bdesign&gclid=CjwKEAiAqMajBRCdjejki6yjuDwSJACQeVukUzfkeDBGnNT4bgU7az_0dDmwhK1-7sMzF5BhC9EsIhoCBwnw_wcB

Useful image libraries:

- Istockphoto. http://www.istockphoto.com/

- Bigstockphoto. http://www.bigstockphoto.com

- Free digital images. http://www.freedigitalimages.net/

- Getty Images, Royalty-free. http://www.gettyimages/royalty-free

- Free Images. http://www.freeimages.com/

- Public Domain pictures. http://www.publicdomainpictures.net/

- Dreamstime. http://www.dreamstime.com/

- Presenter media. http://www.presentermedia.com/

Useful tools for generating graphics

1. Generate a colour pallete from an image. http://bighugelabs.com/colors.php

- Wordle word cloud generator. http://www.wordle.net/

- Tagxedo word cloud generator with shapes. http://www.tagxedo.com/

- ShapeCollage creating digital collages. http://www.shapecollage.com/

- Creating digital Polaroid pictures. http://www.poladroid.net/

- Screencast on how to create sticky tape graphics, http://www.screenr.com/aGh

- Screencast on how to create curly edged shadows. http://www.screenr.com/pV8

- Create your own Motivational Posters. http://bighugelabs.com/motivator.php

- Create your own Keep Calm Posters. http://www.keepcalm-o-matic.co.uk/

- Want to create a cartoon Avatar? http://download.mywebface.com/index.jhtml I find that many people don't like putting their picture up on community sites, but rather than have no picture, I encourage them to create their own avatar. Illustmaker is another good tool for this. http://illustmaker.abi-station.com/index_en.shtml

Useful tools for screen scraping

- *Just be aware of copyright!*

- Snagit. http://www.techsmith.com/snagit.html

- Pixlr. http://apps.pixlr.com/editor/

- Snippy. http://www.softpedia.com/get/Multimedia/Graphic/Graphic-Capture/Snippy.shtml

- Greenshot. http://getgreenshot.org/

- ScreenRip. http://www.snapfiles.com/get/screenrip.html

Books

Draught Associates, *Visual Aid*, Black Dog Publishing Limited, 2008

Dirksen K, *Design for how people learn*, New Riders, Berkeley CA, 2012

Colvin Clark, R., Lyons C., *Graphics for Learning, 2nd Edition*, John Wiley and Sons, 2011

SYNCHRONOUS ENVIRONMENTS RESOURCES

Being able to transferring your teaching/training skills from the classroom to a synchronous environment is becoming a requirement for teachers/trainers. Your ability to engage with your students remains vital, but being confident and competent in your chosen synchronous environment will provide a better experience for you and your students. You'll find the resources in *#EdTechMix2*.

- Colin Steed's definitive book on how to deliver learning using live meetings/webinars

- Roger Corville's Virtual Presenters handbook. http://thevirtualpresenter.com/products/

- This Citrix best practice guide is platform specific, but the guidance can be transferred to any online synchronous environment.
  http://support.citrixonline.com/servlet/fileField?retURL=%2Fapex%2FCPDownloadStarter%3FarticleLinkId%3DGTTD00001%26I%3Den_US%26product%3Dgototraining&entityId=ka35000000OTROdAAO&field=Content__Body__s

- For courses take a look at the LPI Certificate in Designing Online Learning and Certified Online Learning Facilitator. http://www.learningandperformanceinstitute.co.uk/

Books

Steed, C. Facilitating *Live Online learning*, Engaged Online Learning Ltd, 2011. http://colinsteed.com/wp/books

Colvin Clark, R, Kwinn A, *The New Virtual Classroom*, John Wiley & Sons, 2007

Murchoch M, Muller T, *The Learning eXplosion*, FranklinCovey Co., 2011

DIGITAL LITERACY RESOURCES

There are a wide variety of free online courses that can help to improve software skills, from YouTube to Lynda.com and everywhere else. A few sites you might find of interest can be found in *#EdTechMix2*.

Online guides, resources and courses

1. Improve your Google use with the Google guide. http://www.googleguide.com/

- Free online public education. http://alison.com/

- BBC online learning. Even though these courses are no longer being updated, they are still very useful. http://www.bbc.co.uk/learning/onlinecourses/#information

- Free online learning courses from the Open University. http://www.open.edu/openlearn/

- Open of course – free online courses. http://www.open-of-course.org/courses/course/index.php?categoryid=16

- An online Encyclopedia. http://www.encyclopedia.com/

- How stuff works. http://www.howstuffworks.com/ A great site for work and life and your children's homework questions!

- So You Wanna: another useful site. http://www.soyouwanna.com/work-business/

- And of course, WikiHow. http://www.wikihow.com/Main-Page

CURATION RESOURCES

With the mass of information available at your fingertips and the fingertips of your students/learners, the ability to actively filter content to discover good sources and resources needs to extend beyond your browser's favourites bar. Check them out in *#EdTechMix3*.

Tools

- Symbaloo is a personal favourite of mine, and a great way to manage and curate web based resources. I create mixes to share with my students and conference delegates rather than providing a mass of links. It even has a separate version for academic use SymbalooEdu making it an essential tool for teaching the value of a personal learning network, as students can share webmixes, exchange links and more. http://www.symbalooedu.com/

- Scoopit!. Sign up and find others who are curating content that you're interested in, then let the content come to you! Share your own curated content too. http://www.scoop.it/

- Pinterest – curation for everyone and every subject. https://uk.pinterest.com/

- Storify is a tool that helps you collect, curate and share your curations. https://storify.com/

- Pearltrees offers collection, curation and sharing. http://www.pearltrees.com/

- The LearnPatch Friday Filter is a lifeline when you're busy and don't have time to keep on top of what's hot in L&D. An essential subscription to a site that curates and feeds out useful relevant content. http://us5.campaign-archive2.com/?u=fc05205996b45a7fb9c4c51ef&id=4a933e7a59&e=6944cf8700

- Trainingzone is another site that curates relevant information about the learning industry. http://www.trainingzone.co.uk/

- Elearning Learning is another curation site for those interested in eLearning. http://feeds2.feedburner.com/ElearningLearningFull

- An Elearningnews offers a helpful worldwide roundup. http://www.elearningnews.net/

MOBILE RESOURCES

You'll find the resources in *#EdTechMix3*.

- A good place to start with understanding mobile for learning is the World Wide Web Consortium standards for mobile web design. http://www.w3.org/standards/webdesign/mobilweb

- Google has a good white paper on mobile design considerations. http://www.google.co.uk/think/multiscreen/whitepaper-sitedesign.html

- A good article on developing a mobile training strategy. http://elearningindustry.com/8-steps-create-develop-effective-mobile-training-strategy

- ADL's mobile learning handbook for instructional designers. https://sites.google.com/a/adlnet.gov/mobile-learning-guide/home/

- A good roundup of some of the mobile and tablet Apps around for education and learning http://bestonlineuniversities.com/favorite-mobile-learning-apps/#more and another curated list that also has some gems on it to explore. http://www.edudemic.com/the-90-best-ios-apps-for-mobile-learning/

Book

Udell C, Woodill G, *Mastering Mobile Learning*, John Wiley & Sons, 2015

AUDIO RESOURCES

Audio has a solid place in the toolset of the Learning Technologist. The use of podcasts has really taken off, but don't forget that audio content is also useful for students with accessible needs, particularly for students with dyslexia and visual impairment. I have found that in the corporate world, lots of business people consider they are "*too busy to read*" learning materials, and my antidote to that is to ask them if they could possibly "listen while they work"?

Asking a busy executive to listen to a podcast rather than the radio when driving to work or commuting on the train, tube, bus, etc., often helps them find a way to engage with the content. Personally, I listen to PDFs, podcasts and other documents I have to read while I'm ironing, cleaning the house etc. What I found is that taking a first pass at the content by listening to it gives me the bigger picture, and then I am more likely to find the time to sit down and read the document again to focus in on the key elements.

If students/workers are failing to complete pre-reading assignments, consider delivering your content in an audio format. You'll find the resources in *#EdTechMix3*.

Tools

- A guide to using Adobe Read Out Loud. https://www.adobe.com/enterprise/accessibility/reader6/sec2.html

- Audacity is free for you to use to Record, Play and edit audio. http://audacity.download-latest.com/

- How to embed audio file in to an MS Word document. http://www.jiscdigitalmedia.ac.uk/guide/audio-feedback-a-how-to-guide

- YaKiToMe: converts text to speech. https://www.yakitome.com/tts/text_to_speech/Welcome-to-YAKiToMe?b=None

Audio resources

- The BBC Podcast Library. http://www.bbc.co.uk/podcasts

- Learn Out Loud – free audio books. http://www.learnoutloud.com/Free-Audio-Video#directory

- Onlignment's guide to creating podcasts. http://onlignment.com/wp-content/uploads/2011/03/A-practical-guide-to-creating-learning-podcasts.pdf

Music

Music forms a big part of my learning delivery. I use music to set a tone, introduce a subject, change the direction of a class discussion and of course add some fun. Two sites that have proved very useful over the years are detailed below. Please make sure you pay attention to the legal stipulations for use of the materials available on the sites:

- TV Theme tunes. http://www.televisiontunes.com/ TV Ad songs. http://m.tvadsongs.com/

Music to study to

- I often play music during study time, and there is a surprising amount of "music to study to" freely available on the web. https://www.youtube.com/watch?v=dGN2lCOHgoI

SHARING / COLLABORATING RESOURCES

Findings ways to help students/workers share their knowledge, skills and experience forms a fundamental part of the informal learning model which continues to embed itself into all learning situations. The resources listed here are just a small selection, and for every web based tool there is most likely a corresponding phone/tablet App. What is listed here is probably the minimum you should be aware of. You will find the resources in *#EdTechMix4*.

Wikis

- Wiki's in Plain English, explained by CommonCraft. https://www.youtube.com/watch?v=-dnL00TdmLY

- Media Wiki, the original basis of Wikipedia. Open Source and free. http://www.mediawiki.org/wiki/MediaWiki

- Wikispaces offers two packages: Education and Corporate. http://www.wikispaces.com/

- PBWorks, a corporate wiki site. http://www.pbworks.com/

Online collaboration platforms

- Google Apps for education. https://www.google.com/edu/products/productivity-tools/

- Yammer: Create your own private micro-blogging community. https://www.yammer.com/

- Ning: Another private social network environment. http://www.ning.com/

- ELGG is an open source social network engine, either download and host it locally, or let them host it for you. http://elgg.org/

- Grou.ps is another hosted social platform. http://grou.ps/home/?ref=introduction

- Blendspace. https://www.blendspace.com/

Blogging

These days it seems everyone has their own blog, but consider using blogs as an online portfolio for your students/learners. On many courses that I teach, I now provide each participant with their own WordPress blog to customise as they will. The students can choose to share their blog with their cohort or blog in private. Often, they all start out blogging in private, but by the end of the first month of study, most switch to sharing their blogs with either the whole cohort or a chosen group. If you are teaching online learning communities, using WordPress blogs in this way is to me a no brainer.

- Overview of blogging from CommonCraft.
  https://www.youtube.com/watch?v=NN2I1pWXjXI&feature=relmfu

- BuddyPress https://wordpress.org/plugins/buddypress/ is part of the WordPress
  https://wordpress.com/ family and provides the ability to build your own social network.

Social Networking

- Overview of Social Networking.
  https://www.youtube.com/watch?v=6a_KF7TYKVc&feature=relmfu

- Overview of Twitter https://www.youtube.com/watch?v=ddO9idmax0o&feature=relmfu Twitter
  http://www.twitter.com, LinkedIn https://www.linkedin.com/

- Manage your social media streams with Hootsuite. https://hootsuite.com/

- Curate and share on your social media streams with Scredible. https://scredible.com/

- Privacy and Social Networking – what happens to your data – a cautionary view.
  https://www.youtube.com/watch?v=X7gWEgHeXcA&feature=BFa&list=FL2gXnUlmZ2X8yLYNG
  -CN9aA&lf=plpp_video

Sharing

- Share presentation slides online – Slideshare. http://www.slideshare.net/

- Photo and video sharing with Flickr. https://www.flickr.com/

- Online collaborative mindmapping. http://www.mindmeister.com/

- File Sharing with DropBox. https://www.dropbox.com/

- Sharing environment and Apps GoogleDocs.
  http://www.google.com/docs/about/?gclid=CjwKEAiAoJmlBRCxjKeizPHVs1ESJAC6cxjUMfSxD-
  8DI-eaylvFM4AvnT7I49fAuLrTecK8SiDXPhoCmlPw_wcB

Books

Jane Hart's books, website and courses provide probably the best resources for
learning about the value of social learning and networking for learning. For a start,
try:

Hart J., Social Learning Handbook, Centre for Learning & Performance Technologies, 2014.
You can download from: http://c4lpt.co.uk/social-learning-handbook-2014/

Qualman E., Socialnomics, John Wiley & Sons, New Jersey, 2009

Shirky C., Here comes everybody, Penguin Group, London, 2008

Blanchard O., Social Media ROI, Pearson Education, Boston, 2011

DESIGNING RESOURCES

Strong design is not reserved just for eLearning. All forms of learning delivery require an understanding of learning design principles, so here is a roundup of resources and strategies that have become established over the years. You'll find the resources in *#EdTechMix4*.

Instructional design

- Analysis, Design, Development, Implementation and Evaluation – ADDIE http://www.learning-theories.com/addie-model.html Alternatively try Donald Clark's view. http://www.sos.net/~donclark/history_isd/addie.html

- Action Mapping is an e-learning design approach from Cathy Moore. It's agile and worth a look. http://cogprints.org/624/1/V11ANSEK.html She also has a version on SlideShare. http://www.slideshare.net/CathyMoore/design-lively-elearning-with-action-mapping?from=ss_embed

- Roger Shank's Goal Based Scenarios. http://cogprints.org/624/1/V11ANSEK.html

- Robert Gagne's Nine events of instruction. http://edutechwiki.unige.ch/en/Nine_events_of_instruction

- Even more models. http://www.instructionaldesigncentral.com/htm/IDC_instructionaldesignmodels.htm

Learning strategies

- Blended Learning. Clive Shepherd talks about blended learning in five episodes:
  Part 1. https://www.youtube.com/watch?v=UBTCvDjxToc&feature=feedlik
  Part 2 https://www.youtube.com/watch?v=G4f3UftM72c&feature=related
  Part 3 https://www.youtube.com/watch?v=SVTgXIcZucg&feature=related
  Part 4 https://www.youtube.com/watch?v=RjrGDmCEHqo&feature=related
  Part 5 https://www.youtube.com/watch?v=mEL90fN9uII&feature=related

- Donald Clark's "don't lecture me!" lecture from 2010. This is over an hour long and makes the case for changing approaches to education. https://www.youtube.com/watch?v=Tbl-xXF8NPY&feature=channel_video_title

- An overview of Heutagogy (self determined learning) http://en.wikipedia.org/wiki/Heutagogy See also useful PDF on the subject.

http://www.avetra.org.au/abstracts_and_papers_2001/Hase-Kenyon_full.pdf

- Charles Jennings talks about the 70:20:10 model.
  https://www.youtube.com/watch?v=FkB0ECkXd_U

- There is also a LinkedIn Group for 70:20:10 Forum, which is regularly updated with developments, case studies and other resources.

- Ken Robinson on Changing Education Paradigms.
  https://www.youtube.com/watch?v=zDZFcDGpL4U

- Nigel Harrison on the problem with "solutioneering" when you are trying to design learning that works. http://www.trainingzone.co.uk/topic/why-do-most-organisations-jump-learning-solutions-too-quickly/156857

- Overview and guidance on applying Bloom's Taxonomy.
  http://epltt.coe.uga.edu/index.php?title=Bloom%27s_Taxonomy

Books

Horton W., *E-Learning by Design*, John Wiley & Sons, San Francisco, 2006 (There is a later release but I don't have it).

Colvin Clark R, Mayer R. E., *E-Learning and the science of instruction*, Third edition, John Wiley & Sons, San Francisco, 2011

Hodell C, *ISD from the ground up*, American Society for Training and Development, 2011

Shepherd C, *The Blended learning cook book*, Second edition, 2008

Vaughan N.D., Cleveland-Innes M, Garrison D.R., *Teaching in Blended Learning Environments*, AU Press, Athabasca University, Edmonton, 2013

Shepherd C, *The new learning architect*, 2011

Hubbard R, *The really useful e-Learning instruction manual*, John Wiley & Sons, 2013

Harrison N, *Improving Employee Performance*, Kogan Page, 2000

Sloman M, *Training in the age of the learner*, Chartered Institute of Personnel and Development, 2003

Solman M, *The E-learning revolution*, Amacom, 2002

Meister J. C., Willyerd K., *The 2020 Workplace*, HarperCollins publishers, 2010

Paine N., *The Learning Challenge*, Kogan Page Limited, 2014

GAMIFICATION / GAMES FOR LEARNING RESOURCES

The best form of research you can do in the use of games in learning is to play computer games. And if you do not "get" gamification, take a look in your wallet or purse and dig out your coffee shop loyalty card, or your hotel rewards card, or your supermarket rewards card –You'll find the resources in *#EdTechMix5*.

- You're already living in a Gamified world.
  https://www.timetag.tv/learningtechnologies/play/22925

- Thoughts on educational games and games for learning. http://game-research.com/index.php/articles/thoughts-on-learning-in-games-and-designing-educational-computer-games/

- An Educational Game Design model. https://www.youtube.com/watch?v=tZ2qWIkrLYw

- Improving the way we design games for learning by examining how popular video games teach.
  http://www.cse.ucla.edu/products/reports/R798.pdf

- The value of narrative in Serious Game development.
  http://www.narratology.net/sites/www.narratology.net/files/ENN%202011%20Sanna-Mari%20%C3%84yr%C3%A4m%C3%B6%20-%20Narrative%20in%20Serious%20or%20Learning%20Game%20Design%20Reseach.pdf

- Feedback loops in Games and Learning.
  http://muzzylane.com/files/Feedback_Loops_and_Learning.pdf

- Thirty games for iPad to explore. http://www.onlinecollegecourses.com/2012/12/02/the-30-best-educational-games-for-the-ipad-adult-edition/

Books

Prensky M, *Digital game-based learning*, Paragon House, 2007

Aldrich C, *The complete guide to simulations and serious Games*, John Wiley & Sons, 2009

Kapp K.M., *The gamification of learning and instruction*, John Wiley & Sons, 2012

Kapp K.M, *The gamification of learning and instruction field book*, John Wiley & Sons, 2014

McGonigal J, *Reality is broken – Why games make us better and how they can change world*, Vintage, 2011

PERFORMANCE SUPPORT RESOURCES

Performance Support is nothing new, but its relevance to the more informal learning models means it is going through considerable changes. You'll find the resources in *#EdTechMix5*.

Videos to watch

- Bob Mosher is a good place to start if you are new to Performance Support. Where to begin with informal learning http://www.clomedia.com/articles/where-to-begin-with-informal-learning and his 5 moments of need https://www.youtube.com/watch?v=Gi5RXjtvPW8 should provide a good overview.

- Elliot Masie's definition of Performance Support. http://masie.com/Performer-Support-Lab/what-is-performer-support.html

- Don Tapscott– Author of Wikinomics – how mass collaboration changes everything. https://www.youtube.com/watch?v=1Rgk7k9qsZI&list=FL2gXnUlmZ2X8yLYNG-CN9aA&index=2&feature=plpp_video

- Why blogging works in education– a perspective from school children. https://www.youtube.com/watch?v=GJRFYnNP0c8&feature=BFa&list=FL2gXnUlmZ2X8yLYNG-CN9aA&lf=plpp_video

- Prof Stephen Heppell, Learning without Frontiers. https://www.youtube.com/watch?v=SbGTI5UN-_o&feature=BFa&list=FL2gXnUlmZ2X8yLYNG-CN9aA&lf=plpp_video

Books

Gottfredson C, Mosher B, *Innovative Performance Support*, McGraw-Hill, 2011

Rossett A, Schafer L, *Job Aids and Performance Support*, John Wiley & Sons, 2007

Qualman E, *Socialnomics*, John Wiley & Sons, 2009

Hart J, *Social Learning Handbook*, Centre for Learning and Performance Technologies, 2011

Shirky C, *Here comes everybody*, Penguin Books, 2008

Pink D H, *The surprising truth about what motivates us*, Canongate Books, 2011

Heath C, Heath D, *Switch*, Random House Business Books, 2011

Shepherd C, *The New Learning Architect*, Onlignment, 2011

Leadbeater C, *We Think*, Profile Books, 2009

Tapscott D, Williams A D, *Wikinomics* Atlantic Books,2006

Blanchard O, *Social Media ROI*, Peason Education Inc, 2011

Meister J C, Willyerd K, *The 2020 Workplace*, Harper Collins Publishers, 2010

Paine N, *The Learning Challenge*, Kogan Page, 2014

LEARNING MANAGEMENT RESOURCES

My view on learning management is that if what you do to "manage" learning does not deliver back the outcomes required by your students or your organization in a form that you can communicate to organization/business leaders, then you need to review your activities. Here are a few links that might enlighten or enrage you, depending on your viewpoint, or inform you of the existence of many different ways of evaluating learning beyond Kirkpatrick. You'll find the resources in *#EdTechMix5*.

- Kirkpatrick 4 levels of evaluation the revised version on the Kirkpatrick website. http://www.kirkpatrickpartners.com/OurPhilosophy/tabid/66/Default.aspx

- Jack Phillips ROI extension of the Kirkpatrick model. http://epiclearninggroup.com/uk/files/2013/11/phillips_evaluation.pdf

- Daniel Stufflebeam CIPP Model, SlideShare explanation. http://www.slideshare.net/oa1994/orly-cipp-model

- Robert Stake Responsive Evaluation Model. http://education.illinois.edu/circe/Publications/Responsive_eval.pdf

- Robert Stake Congruence-Contingency Model/ Countenance Model. http://education.illinois.edu/circe/Publications/countenance.pdf

- Kaufman's Five Levels of Evaluation. http://home.gwu.edu/~rwatkins/articles/whatwork.PDF

- CIRO- Context Input Reaction Outcome. https://books.google.co.uk/books?id=LWQHgiFpr8wC&pg=PA330&lpg=PA330&dq=The+CIRO+four-level+approach+was+developed+by+Warr,+Bird+and+Rackham+%281970%29.&source=bl&ots=TLG0_Q5uX0&sig=ISULJ456dYixaOTotSUrUq17XFw&hl=en&sa=X&ei=FNSnVJ3jAuiU7QbGtoDQCw&ved=0CCEQ6AEwAA#v=onepage&q=The%20CIRO%20four-level%20approach%20was%20developed%20by%20Warr%2C%20Bird%20and%20Rackham%20(1970).&f=false

- PERT- Programme Evaluation and Review Technique. http://en.wikipedia.org/wiki/Program_evaluation_and_review_technique

- Marvin Alkins on the Development of Evaluation theory. https://www.cse.ucla.edu/products/evaluation/cresst_ec1969_o.pdf

- Michael Scriven – The logic of Evaluation. http://www.rismes.it/pdf/Scriven_Logic_evaluation.pdf

- A guide to Porvus Discrepancy Model. http://acrs.org.au/files/arsrpe/RS000047.pdf

- Eisner's Educational Connoisseurship and Criticism model.
  http://www.tojqi.net/articles/TOJQI_1_2/TOJQI_1_2_Article_6.pdf

- Illuminative Evaluation Model – see Section B and C of this paper.
  http://www.enquirylearning.net/ELU/Issues/Research/Res1Ch6.html

- The future of e-assessment – a BILD white paper,
  http://www.towardsmaturity.org/article/2011/04/04/bild-future-e-assessment/

- B R Worthen Goal Free Evaluation. http://legacy.oise.utoronto.ca/research/field-centres/ross/ctl1014/Worthen1990.pdf

CONTINUOUS PROFESSIONAL DEVELOPMENT RESOURCES

You'll find the resources in *#EdTechMix5*.

- An overview of Continuous Professional development. http://www.jobs.ac.uk/careers-advice/managing-your-career/1318/what-is-continuing-professional-development-cpd

- Interactive CPD Toolkit. http://www.jobs.ac.uk/careers-advice/resources/ebooks-and-toolkits/interactive-cpd-toolkit/

- Martyn Sloman's L&D 2020 A guide for the next decade.
  http://www.martynsloman.co.uk/ld2020.pdf

- Towards Maturity – a wide range of useful resources, papers and events.
  http://www.towardsmaturity.org/

- Jane Hart's Directory of Learning and Performance Tools. http://c4lpt.co.uk/directory-of-learning-performance-tools/ Also check out her Top 100 tools for the current year.

- Go2Web20 http://www.go2web20.net/ a wide range of online tools and applications.

CONCLUSION

Being a Learning Technologist is not an elite role. Every teacher and trainer needs to become their own Learning Technologist, developing knowledge and skills with learning technology that they can apply to their specific teaching environment(s), selecting technology that works within their budget and is appropriate to their students/learners needs.

Staying on top of the emerging trends in tools, strategies and emerging developments takes effort, but it is possible by harnessing the worldwide network of learning professionals who are passionate about the subject and are actively sharing their findings, research, successes and failures. We are living through a prolonged and fundamental shift in our understanding of how humans learn and develop – there truly has never been such an exciting time to be in education/learning and development.

CITATION

Wedgwood, J. (2015). The skills and knowledge of a Learning Technologist. In: Hopkins, D., ed., *The Really Useful #EdTechBook*, 1st ed. David Hopkins, pp.61-90.

LEARNING TECHNOLOGIST AS DIGITAL PEDAGOGUE

DR. DAVID WALKER & SHEILA MACNEILL

Dr. David Walker, Head of Technology Enhanced Learning, University of Sussex

@drdjwalker

http://blogs.sussex.ac.uk/tel

Dr David Walker has responsibility for informing strategic institutional approaches and developments in the use of technology in teaching and learning at the University of Sussex. Prior to joining Sussex in 2013 he was Senior Learning Technologist at the University of Dundee and Visiting Lecturer in Technology Enhanced Learning at Edinburgh Napier University. David is a member of the Executive Committee of the Staff and Educational Development Association (SEDA), Co-Chair of the SEDA Conference Committee and a member of the UCISA Academic Support Group. He represents Sussex on the UK Heads of eLearning Forum (HeLF) and Heads of Educational Development Group (HEDG) and is an editor of the Journal of Perspectives in Applied Academic Practice (JPAAP).

Sheila MacNeill, Senior Lecturer in Blended Learning, Glasgow Caledonian University

@sheilmcn

http://howsheilaseesit.wordpress.com/

Sheila MacNeill is a Senior Lecturer in Blended Learning at Glasgow Caledonian University. Working in learning technology for over 15 years Sheila has progressed from a Learning Technologist to her current role, working at both institutional and sectoral levels. A highlight of Sheila's career was being awarded the ALT Learning Technologist of the Year Award in 2013. Sheila is now also a Trustee of ALT. A committed open practitioner Sheila regularly shares her thoughts and experiences on all aspects of learning and teaching using technology on her blog.

INTRODUCTION

What are the distinguishing characteristics of a Learning Technologist, those qualities that serve to identify them and differentiate them from other roles?

The role of the Learning Technologist is, it is fair to say, ill defined. The question of professional identity has long vexed many working in the field of learning technology with debate surrounding the attributes, values, requisite skills and experiences associated with our conceptual understanding of the role. The factors that influence the way Learning Technologists perceive their role are many, though the varied professional locations in which they are situated - a topic addressed within another chapter of this book - have been found to shape perspectives on the role and its associated activities (Ellaway, Dewhurst, Begg & MacLeod, 2006).

Martin Oliver was one of the first to attempt to address the role of these 'emerging professionals' back in 2002 acknowledging a *"...growing group whose practices are poorly understood, even within their own community"* (2002, p. 245). Oliver identified five fundamental areas of practice relating to the work of Learning Technologists based on a qualitative study examining descriptions of the role at that time:

1.   Centering on collaborative curriculum development, usually initiated by an academic and focused on a particular piece of technology;
2.   Typically including additional administrative, technical, research or management functions;
3.   Being educative, using discussion, case studies and problems within the

context of collaborations as the basis for reflection, and seeking to move the academic from the particular issues of implementation to more general educational issues;

4.   Being situated, drawing on the idea of communities of practice, and thus requiring the Learning Technologist to learn as well as teach during collaboration;

5.   Being responsible but without authority, relying on goodwill, expertise and rhetoric to create opportunities (both practical and educational) and influence policy.

In the period that has followed the learning/educational technology community has expanded rapidly and many of those early career Learning Technologists, regarded by Conole (2014) to be among the first generation, are now in senior positions - spread across a variety of departmental locations - and increasingly with responsibility for developing and actioning learning and teaching strategies and frameworks.

In this chapter, using the five areas of practice identified by Oliver as a starting point, we hope to be able to open up another discussion about the development, recognition and professionalisation of Learning Technologists within the higher education (HE) context. To chart this journey, including the key milestones which have shaped the very notion of what it is to be a Learning Technologist, we plan to use three key questions, the answers to which we feel will help solidify views around not just what a Learning Technologist does, but why and what they represent.

1.   What makes a Learning Technologist and how does the role differ from those working in IT Support, the Library or Careers?

2.   What are the distinguishing characteristics of a Learning Technologist?

3.   Is there something fundamental that distinguishes Learning Technologists from educational developers? Do we still need both roles?

Crucially, as well as drawing upon our own experiences and relevant research, we have sought answers from the learning technology community both in the UK and beyond. The immediacy of the response and the depth of engagement exemplified the collegiate nature of a professional learning network. It also demonstrated a high level of self-reflective practice and willingness to collectively share and develop understanding of professional identity - across a variety of roles - within that network.

WHAT MAKES A LEARNING TECHNOLOGIST AND HOW DOES THE ROLE DIFFER FROM THOSE WORKING IN IT SUPPORT, THE LIBRARY OR CAREERS?

Our answers to this question are shaped significantly by our similar professional experiences which have enabled us to reflect on this from the different perspectives and levels we have occupied throughout our careers. It is fair to say that when we applied for positions as Learning Technologists over 10 years ago neither of us were really familiar with the job title or even what the role entailed. It was the time of learning objects, VLEs were the new thing - SCORM, content packaging and metadata were going to allow us to share everything. Learning Design was going to put pedagogy before technology. The role itself was a curiosity and it served (and hopefully continues to serve) to be curious. A strong practical dimension underpinned our activities, working on a range of projects from developing games for language learning, multimedia projects and online assessment development, to online events using the VLE. Our work however often took us beyond the provision of technical support and content development to working in partnership with academics to explore ways in which resources or learning opportunities might be designed, enhanced or re-conceptualised in ways which supported a closer alignment with desired learning outcomes.

A systems sensibility combined with an awareness of the appropriateness of different technologies in different disciplinary contexts, is viewed by Learning Technologists as insufficient for the satisfactory fulfillment of the the role. Learning Technologists need a firm grounding in the principles of curriculum design, authentic learning activities, assessment and feedback as well as their own institutional policies, politics and structures. Fox and Sumner (2014) support this view asserting that *"The skill set and experience required has expanded"* (p.101).

94

Increasingly, effective Learning Technologists' skillfully traverse the technological and pedagogical domains, shifting across and combining the two as each learning and teaching situation demands. This perception, along with some alternative viewpoints, was echoed in comments we received in response to our blog post.

> "...Learning Technologists have (or should have) a much better understanding of the teaching/learning context and can see the bigger picture of how a technology can be used to support that. For IT support, the focus is the technology. As Learning Technologists, the technology should never be the focus – good pedagogy is paramount. Moreover, we have to be able to identify where technology won't help. Library staff, in contrast, have more of a focus on providing discipline specific information/content and access to this. Again, there is less focus on pedagogy." (Sharon Flynn)

However there is acknowledgement that in some areas the professional activities of Learning Technologists overlaps with other roles.

> "Although there may be subtle differences in the focus of the LT across different sectors of a HE organisation, I believe we are now seeing a convergence of approaches and responsibilities. This may not hold in all organisations with centralised/localised support models, but there is a greater expectation for IT Teams to be directly supporting academic staff, library staff being involved in eLearning projects and careers publishing online training courses." (John Couperthwaite)

That subtle difference in the nature of the support given by Learning Technologists, particularly in terms of their relationship with academics, seems to us to be crucial in differentiating between roles. The Learning Technologist role is less about making the technology work and more about making the individual (the academic, the student) work (or in an educational context teach and/or learn) more effectively.

> "when I am talking to staff and want to quickly (and flippantly?) explain the difference between me and an IT technician - 'If the technology is broken,

you want to talk to IT. If you are broken, ring me.'" (Joseph Gliddon)

WHAT ARE THE DISTINGUISHING CHARACTERISTICS OF A LEARNING TECHNOLOGIST?

Of all the questions we asked this one seemed to prove the most challenging with the majority of responses failing to identify characteristics associated with the role of a Learning Technologists that could be described as truly distinguishing. Most focussed on the qualities deemed to be desirable in a Learning Technologist. This may be due to the historically wide range of academic and professional disciplines from which many Learning Technologists have originated and the continuing variation in job descriptions, grade and specialisms across the sector.

> *"...being attentive, creative, helpful and a good communicator are essential" (John Couperthwaite)*

> *"You need to be adaptable" (David Hopkins)*

However, socially located (digital) literacies did emerge as one distinguishably distinctive characteristic.

> *"Disciplinary practices intimates that a literacies perspective is also required. That is, an understanding of the social, situated and technical nature of digital technology use; technology uses are at heart are literacy practices. Literacy practices (digital literacies) are highly contextual. They implicate meaning making for a community or an individual and they embed their values and beliefs. I think a Learning Technologist must also have a solid understanding of literacy as social practice in order to help communities and individuals with the adoption of appropriate technology" (Helen Crump)*

This would appear to reinforce the need of Learning Technologists to have an awareness of disciplinary pedagogies and practices and to establish a shared dialogue with the various constituents within a learning community.

96

IS THERE SOMETHING FUNDAMENTAL THAT DISTINGUISHES LEARNING TECHNOLOGISTS FROM EDUCATIONAL DEVELOPERS? DO WE STILL NEED BOTH ROLES?

In our response to these overarching questions, we raised further questions around the evolving role and professionalisation of the Learning Technologist over the past decade. We were again primarily driven by our own career progression, but were also trying to reflect upon the changes we have seen within our peer group and sectoral developments. The additional questions we raised were:

- Is there something fundamental that distinguishes Learning Technologists from educational developers? Do we still need both roles?
- If a fundamental part of the role of a Learning Technologist is their knowledge of educational design practice then should we be evolving into educational developers, or is this still a distinct discipline?
- As Learning Technology Advisors, Learning Architects etc emerge does anyone really know?
- As more "senior" Learning Technologists take up more senior positions within larger departments/directorates (that often include librarians, educational developers and Learning Technologists working side-by-side) and are responsible for developing and actioning learning and teaching strategies/frameworks and increasing the quantity and quality research, does it really matter?
- Are we just grappling with the same issues but with a bit of TEL goodness thrown into the mix?
- Is TEL research mature enough to be seen as distinct from traditional educational development research, and should it continue to be so?

As the roles and people have matured the community has become established and professionalised within the sector, "Learning Technologist" is now a recognised career option with defined progression points such as Senior Learning Technologist within nationally recognised pay and grading schemes. This contrasts starkly and positively with the situation in 2000 when the so called new specialists had little or no formal professional development opportunities (Beetham, 2000) and instead were more likely to develop skills in ad-hoc, just in time ways. Alongside the more traditional Masters in Education there are now a variety of specialist qualifications focusing on the role of technology in education, many of which also carry professional accreditation of varying forms.

The formation and growth of the Association for Learning Technology (ALT) in the UK, and similar bodies such as Ascilite in Australia, have provided a focus not only for developing scholarly activity through conferences and publications, but perhaps more importantly through the development of a professional, peer reviewed, portfolio based, accreditation programme CMALT (Certified Member of ALT). ALT now provides a recognised voice for public consultation on cross-sectoral developments relating to Technology Enhanced Learning. The Staff and Educational Development Association (SEDA) through their Professional Development Framework has also provided recognition of Technology Enhanced Learning for a number of years with awards such as Embedding Learning Technologies and Supporting Learning with Technology.

Another key milestone in the professionalisation of the role of the Learning Technologist, and acknowledgement of the roles increasing significance in pedagogical design processes, became apparent with the launch of the Higher Education Academy's revised UK Professional Standards Framework in 2011.

The updated framework – a set of professional standards for the HE sector to facilitate benchmarking and align professional development provision – emphasised the need to afford greater recognition to the role of emerging technologies, and importantly, the need to extend opportunities to undertake teaching qualifications to all staff working in HE with teaching responsibilities.

The wider recognition of those who provide significant input to the process of supporting teaching and learning ensures that individuals, such as Learning Technologists, are able to access and engage with relevant development opportunities – such as Postgraduate Certificates in Higher Education.

By acknowledging the wider array of stakeholders who contribute to the educational environment and student experience, the revised framework offered the potential for institutions to align the professional values and practices of those actively engaged in teaching and learning. For Learning Technologists, the revised framework provided a basis against which to evidence their professionalism (for career progression, reward or other forms of recognition) and a mechanism to guide their ongoing personal and professional development.

Alongside these positive developments, from the responses to our blog post it would appear that there are still underlying concerns about the division of labour with the sector and the need to have distinctly recognised skill sets and job titles.

> *"My practical and research experience with LTech just reinforces for me the dangers of the split between users and developers/implementers. Even the terms are wrong as it is teachers who 'implement' pedagogy in sociotechnical contexts." (Frances Bell)*

> *"Yes there is, and yes we should have both roles." (John Couperthwaite)*

> *" . . .sitting between (or over arching) the two fields of TEL and Educational Development is that of literacies. Might a sign of maturity be closer recognition of the inter relatedness of all three fields?" (Helen Crump)*

However there is also recognition of the need to enable more team based approaches and in the simplest terms to "get stuff done". In some ways the actual job title doesn't matter.

> *"I do not see the need to dilute what we do by having multiple titles for our roles – my current role is an eLearning Consultant (effectively a Senior Learning Technologist). In a Business School this title is more aligned to a business environment, but it could have other historical reasons. if we are indeed sharing many responsibilities and approaches (less 'click-this' and more 'this is why you may want to click-this') then the more the individual*

titles are meaningless. (David Hopkins)"

The Learning Technologist as enabler of change and a bridge between technology, people and curriculum is something that appears to be part of the professional DNA of a Learning Technologist. The 'bridge' analogy is something we also alluded to in our blog post when we asked:

> *"As our digital and physical learning environments continue to evolve, are we now seeing the need for new a hub/space with people that work there providing effective bridges between traditional spaces such as disciplines, educational development, developing digital literacies, the curriculum, research, staff and students?"*

Again this did seem to resonate.

> *"I'd agree with David [Hopkins] that this is about what you do rather than what you are called, and the difficulty in defining this is what causes confusion. When I tried to follow this through, I wandered down thinking about the process by which many 'Learning Technologists'/'digital pedagogues' arrive in the role: it could be viewed as being through going beyond a single discipline and bridging to a co-existing discipline in order to make them complementary. That is, the role is about bridging and thereby allowing those/knowledge on either side of the divide to reach each other; it's translating for the different disciplines, but also about understanding both so as to recognise and harness the emergent properties from the meeting of disciplines." (Paige Cuffe)*

The jury seems to be out around the idea that the next evolutionary stage of the Learning Technologist is to that of a digital pedagogue.

> *"yeah, gotta think this through. Also,is there such a thing as a digital heutagogue, I wonder." @crumphelen:*

> *@sheilmcn: @crumphelen very probably" < digital nomads? @penpln*

> *@penpln @sheilmcn possibly. Digital heutagogue > a digitally literate,*
> *self-determined learner. Know any??? (@crumphelen)*

Whilst the notion did resonate with some, there were valuable expressions of concern including one relating to wider economic rationales around increased division of labour.

> *". . . there remains a need in academic institutions for dedicated staff to*
> *make sense of the confusion surrounding integration, usability, security,*
> *and application." (John Couperthwaite)*

> *"I'll have to give this some more thought but it occurs to me that the 'prof*
> *services' academic split that I have observed in HE orgs may be designed*
> */ facilitate increasing 'outsourcing' of teaching function, enabling devaluing*
> *of human aspects, diverting education cash to tech companies." (Frances*
> *Bell)*

This latter point is out of scope for this chapter and indeed was something that did not emerge in our scoping discussions. Given the current uncertainty of funding and sustainability and pressures within the education sector and the wider economy this is something that we should all be cognisant of.

CONCLUSION

Over the past two decades there has been significant progress in the recognition and development of the role of the Learning Technologist. Reflecting on Oliver's conclusions around the question of what does a Learning Technologist do, we suggest that there have been significant advances and recognition of the central role that the Learning Technologist plays particularly in relation to collaborative curriculum development, networking, scholarly activities and increasingly recognised influence in the development and implementation of institutional, and indeed sectoral, strategic goals relating to learning and teaching.

Table 1 highlights what we believe the key differences are between Learning Technologists in 2002 and 2014. At the turn of the century, we were described as the "new professionals". The people who had moved from many different disciplines and professions into the realm of learning technology. In the past 14 years, it is clear that these new professionals have become a far more situated, recognised and confident group.

2002 (Oliver)	2014 (Walker, MacNeill)
centring on collaborative curriculum development, usually initiated by an academic and focused on a particular piece of technology	centring on collaborative curriculum development, based on a collaborative team based approach including academics, other support services and students, focused on achieving particular strategic learning and teaching goals.
typically including additional administrative, technical, research or management functions	typically including additional administrative, technical, scholarly activities, public engagement/outreach, research or management functions
being educative, using discussion, case studies and problems within the context of collaborations as the basis for reflection, and seeking to move the academic from the particular issues of implementation to more general educational issues	moving from issues of implementation to more holistic discussions around designing and embedding within curricula.
being situated, drawing on the idea of communities of practice, and thus requiring the Learning Technologist to learn as well as teach during collaboration;	immersed within personal learning networks connecting and connected with global educators in a global community of practice as part of an ongoing process of professional development and peer support.
being responsible but without authority,	Professional recognition of expertise

relying on goodwill, expertise and rhetoric to create opportunities (both practical and educational) and influence policy	resulting in enhanced authority and input into development and implementation of institutional/sectoral policies and strategies

Table 1: Changing characteristics of Learning Technologists

However, we do feel that there could be a flip side to this increased professionalism. Many people, including ourselves, perhaps fell into learning technology as opposed to it being a viable or even imaginable career choice. If we close down the definition of a Learning Technologist too much, are we in danger of creating job descriptions and institutional expectations that Learning Technologists are no more that glorified button pushers who only "know about the VLE"? In making our practice more explicit and compartmentalised is there a danger that we negate the emergent potential of the role by constraining and overly defining areas of work?

Whilst the increasing professionalism and enhanced career prospects of Learning Technologists are to be welcomed, some of the diversity of experiences and outlook those first generation Learning Technologists brought to the role may be lost. However, the response our pre-chapter blog post created would indicate that there is still a vibrancy and creativity within the broad spectrum of the learning technology community and our personal/professional networks. It is also clear is that there are many perhaps now "not so new professionals" who clearly align and situate themselves within the wider learning technology community without having the job title of Learning Technologist.

In the light of ongoing discussions we propose that the 'new professionals' of 2015 are an emerging tribe of digital pedagogues with focus on learning enhancement and advocacy of innovative practices underpinned by research and scholarly activities. Among this overlapping community of professionals, we would argue that Learning Technologists - operating across academic disciplines, support services and more senior management positions - with their ability to engage in discussions with colleagues from multiple disciplines beyond simply the use of technology identifies them as our most rounded pedagogues. If, as has been suggested, we are now entering a post digital age, educational development within a narrow horizon focussing on one particular specialism will not adequately serve the needs of learners, institutions, employers or society.

REFERENCES

Beetham, H (2000) Career Development of Learning Technology Staff: Scoping Study Final Report http://www.jisc.ac.uk/media/documents/programmes/jos/cdss_final_report_v8.pdf accessed, November 2014.

Conole, G. 2004. The role of learning technology practitioners and researchers in understanding networked learning. Proceedings of the Networked Learning Conference 2004, Lancaster University, UK. Available online at http://www.networkedlearningconference.org.uk/past/nlc2004/proceedings/symposia/symposium1/conole.htm [Accessed 2nd Dec. 2014]

Ellaway, R., Begg, M., Dewhurst, D., and MacLeod, H. (2006) In a Glass Darkly: identity, agency and the role of the learning technologist in shaping the learning environment. E-learning. 3(1), 75-87.

Fox , O. & Sumner, N. (2014) Analyzing the Roles, Activities, and Skills of Learning Technologists: A Case Study From City University London, American Journal of Distance Education, 28:2, 92-102.

Oliver, M. (2002) What do Learning Technologists Do? Innovations in Education and Training International, 39 (4), 245-252.

MacNeill, S., Walker, D, Is there something about Learning Technologists? https://howsheilaseesit.wordpress.com/2014/10/10/is-there-something-about-learning-technologists-edtechbook/ blog post, 10 October 2014.

ADDITIONAL RESOURCES

Collated Twitter responses to the blog post https://storify.com/sheilmcn/what-is-it-about-learning-technologists

ACKNOWLEDGEMENTS

We would like to thank everyone who commented on our initial blog post and shared their views with us on Twitter. We were delighted with the level of engagement we received. We couldn't include all the quotes in the chapter but we hope that the ones we have used are representative. As we were writing this chapter, there were a number of parallel discussions taking place on the ALT mailing list, which helped to affirm our position. We would also like to thank Professor Keith Smyth (University of the Highlands and Islands), Professor Linda Creanor and Jim Emery (both Glasgow Caledonian University) for being informal sounding boards and reviewing our chapter.

CITATION

Walker, D. and MacNeill, S (2015). Learning Technologist as Digital Pedagogue. In: Hopkins, D., ed., *The Really Useful #EdTechBook*, 1st ed. David Hopkins, pp.91-105.

TIMES THEY ARE A CHANGING … OR NOT?

LESLEY PRICE

CEO, Learn Appeal

@lesleywprice

http://www.learnappeal.com

Lesley's passion for learning began 30 years ago in 1985 when she started lecturing in FE. She has always been interested in technology and the mid 1990's, realised its potential to support and enhance learning. Since then Lesley has been responsible for regional and national eLearning initiatives in both the education and corporate environments. During her career she has worked in senior roles for the JISC, Becta, the Learning and Performance Institute and, following her recent retirement, is now working part-time as CEO of Learn Appeal.

EARLY DAYS (1969-1974)

I have always been interested in technology. As a child, I used to love going to my father's office because I was allowed to 'play' with the typewriters. Imagine my delight when, as an eleven year old, I was given a typewriter for Christmas…and not a children's 'Petite Typewriter' either, it was the real thing – a full size Olivetti! Within a few months, I wouldn't say that I was perfect at touch typing, but I knew my way around the keyboard and could type without mistakes.

As a teenager, my enjoyment of visits to the office continued as it meant I could spend time either with the punch-card or telex operators. I was absolutely fascinated that cards with holes in them actually stored information and that a long stream of tape, also with holes, could send messages in real time that could be printed anywhere in the world that also had a telex. When I look back, I am amazed that the operators were so patient with me. They not only patiently answered my endless questions, they actually showed me how to use their machines and let me create my own punch cards and also send telexes.

The lessons I learned:

- *Encourage people to play with technology - but in a safe environment.*
- *If people are interested in what you are doing with technology, spend time explaining it and if possible allow them to try it out for themselves.*

GETTING 'HANDS ON' WITH COMPUTERS (1974-1976)

Although I had the qualifications to go to University, I didn't really know what I wanted to do, so I looked for work instead. With a deep interest in technology still driving me, I got a job as a computer operator in the Investment Department of Prudential Assurance. I wish I had taken photographs of the 'computer' - or microcomputer, as it was called. It had a very simple processor with an integral keyboard and no VDU - just a very small 'screen area' above the processor unit big enough to show two or three lines of text. It was connected to a double cassette unit; one cassette stored the program and the other data. As for the printer, it was an IBM Selectric ('golf ball') typewriter which at the time was regarded as being 'state of the art'.

Although very basic, the microcomputer was a real step forward for the Investment Department; its implementation served a business-critical need and was supported 100% by senior management. Investment Analysts were responsible for deciding which shares should be bought and how these shares should be allocated to the appropriate fund. To do this, analysts spent their time reviewing share prices and calculating yields before purchasing on behalf of the company, as well as looking at overall fund performance. At the end of every day, monies not invested in funds were deposited overnight with those banks offering the best rate. Weekly and monthly reports were produced on all fund performance.

Before the microcomputer, all calculations were done by the analysts, using comptometers. Calculations were hand-written and reports produced by the typing pool. This was very time-consuming for analysts and typists alike. On the other hand, the microcomputer could produce yield calculations, fund valuations and reports, all at the press of a button.

The outcome was a 'win-win' for everyone. Typists did not have to spend hours transcribing hand-written notes and analysts had more time to focus on their key role, while senior managers could demonstrate more effective use of staff resource.

I had ambitions way beyond being a computer operator, so then went to University. After that, I was accepted onto the ICL (International Computers Limited) Technical Support Graduate Programme. However, things did not turn out as planned. ICL customers wanted to avoid their systems being shut down or disrupted during working hours which meant, unless I was assigned to a new installation, a great deal of evening and weekend work. I therefore decided to leave and pursue a different career, which did not involve technology.

I spent the next four years as an Office Manager in a sales office for an American company involved in the oil industry. In the 80's this part of the Scottish economy was booming, but it was also incredibly competitive. We kept detailed records on all our customers so that we could track sales and anticipate their needs. My Regional Manager was a hard taskmaster. He was very experienced, a stickler for detail and knew exactly what was required to win business. He constantly repeated that a good product in itself is not enough - building customer relationships on both a business and social level is what wins orders. He also taught me not to make assumptions. One of his stock phrases, which I still quote regularly is: "*Don't assume as it makes an ASS out of U and ME.*"

The lessons I learned:

- *Technology is more likely to succeed if it fulfills a clear business need.*
- *Senior management needs to see and understand these benefits.*
- *Providing and demonstrating a WIIFM (What's In It For Me) to all staff will build support rather than create barriers.*

- *Building relationships takes time but pays dividends.*
- *Don't make assumptions, especially when people are involved, by seeing things from your perspective rather than theirs.*

LEARNING AND TECHNOLOGY COMING TOGETHER (1985-1998)

As with most people, my journey into learning was serendipitous – it was most definitely by accident rather than design. By 1985, I had a young family and was seeking a job that would give me more flexibility, so I became a 'part time lecturer' at Loughborough College.

Back then, technology was not an integral part of FE learning unless you worked in Computer Studies. There was limited availability of Computer Based Training (CBT), but it was only used if there was software available that could be bought and stored locally. Floppy discs could not hold much data in those days and CD-ROMs were not invented until 1984. Some colleges, including Loughborough, had 'interactive video labs' where students could learn using 12" LaserDiscs. However the range of content was very limited and was always seen as an add-on to the curriculum, rather than part of the learning process.

It's probably worth remembering how much impact technology has had, not just on learning, but on preparation and general administration. During my first twelve years in FE, everything we did was very 'low tech'. Most worksheets were hand written and run-off on Banda Machines. Can you still remember the smell? At Loughborough College, if you wanted a more professional 'look and feel' it depended on whether you could type or not. If you could, you were able to print documents, fill in a photocopy request form and take them to the 'repro office'. The alternative was to type onto 'stencils' which were then duplicated using either a Roneo or Gestetner machine. If you couldn't type - and that was the case for most FE lecturers - you submitted hand written documents to either the secretaries or the training office for typing and then 'duplication'.

This palaver meant that you had to be well prepared. I taught Applied Business Economics and Marketing and there many times when I wanted to include additional information about political or economic events, which I felt, were relevant and that often meant changing hand-outs at the last minute. I can still remember the morning queues outside the 'repro office' where members of staff from various departments were waiting to get hand-outs either photocopied or run off on the Banda. Whilst very inconvenient, these queues were actually water-cooler opportunities for me to talk to members of staff from other departments. While we were waiting, we chatted about the resources we were getting printed, why they were important to our learners and why we were rushing at the last moment. These brief dialogues with colleagues who worked in a different area were actually great networking opportunities.

Loughborough College was particularly forward looking and, by 1998, staff and students alike had improved access to both computers and the Internet. The library had become a Learning Resource Centre (LRC) and there had been significant investment in both technology and IT support. The college had a robust network, server capacity to store resources and (due to its proximity to Loughborough University) a JANET connection, which provided broadband Internet access across the network.

Looking back, 1998 was my personal 'tipping point'. Over the years I had watched my daughter, Natalie, using the computer. She particularly liked Encarta and had a natural curiosity in discovery that we so often see in children. Using Encarta, Natalie increased not only her depth of knowledge but also her understanding of a topic she was covering in school. She would come home, look it up and then spend hours clicking links to find related information. We were early adopters of the Internet and to help her with her homework I set her puzzles and challenges. She also regularly played 'Where in the World is Carmen Sandiego' (1), an educational game where she collected clues and learned about different countries.

That year, just before the school holidays, Natalie (then thirteen) had decided that she wanted to use the Internet to create a personalised 'information pack' for each one of her friends, about their pets. Over the summer, she learned how to identify useful resources, cut and paste images and text as well as how to spell-check documents. The packs she created included photographs, feeding habits and all

111

kinds of other things about pets, which she thought would interest her friends. When she returned to school at the end of the holidays, Natalie gave each of her friends their present - a printed copy of the information pack about their pet. Each one had a photograph of the friend and their animal on the front page....it was truly personalised. As an aside, it may come as no surprise to learn that Natalie is now a primary school teacher and she uses the skills she learned that summer, every day in her working life.

I learned a lot from my daughter while she was carrying out her self-assigned project. One of my greatest challenges in FE was teaching mixed ability groups and the need for differentiation. Some students grasped concepts really quickly; their knowledge and understanding needed to be extended, whilst others required re-enforcement. This was made possible through worksheets, getting students to do further research in the library or by setting them a task using the Internet. However, worksheets took time to produce and carrying out research in the library was useful - but neither activity was particularly stimulating. The students enjoyed finding out more about the topic using the Internet, but much like today, it could be like looking for needle in a haystack.

I wanted to create interesting Internet activities for my students that would provide both extension and re-enforcement of their knowledge and understanding. The challenge was how to achieve this. I had no idea about computer programming languages and HTML was way over my head, so I started doing my own research and found out about an organisation called NILTA (National Information Learning Technologies Association (2)). I attended one of their events and met with other FE practitioners who were creating webpages and resources to support learning. This event was a 'light bulb' moment as I found out that I didn't have to know how to write coding, there were software programs that could do it for me. I called into PC World on the way home and bought MS FrontPage.

The lessons I learned:

- *It often takes what might seem a set of unrelated events and circumstances to align and create the 'perfect storm'*

- *Watch and learn from how children interact and use technology. They are using it because they want to, not because they have to.*
- *When content is personalised, it makes it real. It can have a positive impact on the provider and receiver as it helps build and strengthen a mutual relationship.*

DUCKS IN A ROW? ALL BOXES TICKED!

On a personal level, between 1985 and 1998, technology progressed and I never lost interest. PCs became more powerful, the Internet was born and I kept pace. My first computer was an Amstrad PCW8512 and from that I went on to a succession of IBMs that used DOS followed by Windows 95 and then Windows 98.

It's when I look back to this point in my learning technologies journey I realise that people are still discussing and trying to resolve many of the issues and barriers that I faced back then. Is history really repeating itself?

Using FrontPage, I taught myself how to create simple web pages that contained content, links and activities. The next step was to make them available to my students. The only way to do this was not only to get the IT support team involved, but get them to 'buy in' to what I wanted to do – so I worked beneath the radar, from bottom-up to top-down and vice versa. I had also learned lessons from my past experience and recognised that I needed a 'three pronged' attack. I needed support not only from the IT support team, but also from the person responsible for Learning Resources in the college and ultimately, if what I was planning was going to have an impact on all students in the college and not just my students, I also needed the College Principal's support.

Although I was not a 'techie', I had kept up with developments as a user. I knew the first step was to get the IT support team on board because they could potentially be blockers rather than enablers. Rather than sending emails, in between my teaching timetable, I spent time talking and listening to the IT support team. This reaped rewards as IT support staff began to understand what I was trying to do. I in turn understood their issues and through this partnership we created an area on the intranet for my students. I created webpages with links to Internet resources. I also used WebQuest *(3)* to create interactive role-play games on the topic we were studying. Today I guess we would call it gamification - and my students loved it.

The next step was to develop the same kind of relationship with the LRC Manager who had line management responsibility for the IT support team who I already had on-side. Again, I was in a fortunate position. The LRC Manager realised that learning technology had the potential to make a step change to the service her department offered to the college and so she invested in a subscription to Infotrac (4). This online resource enabled me to create, what we would call today, 'curated' content. Using one link on a webpage, I was able to direct students to a range of resources that was updated automatically and was relevant to the subject we were covering at the time.

The next step was to convince the college Principal, Jim Mutton, that learning technologies offered huge potential to students, staff and the college. I hate to think how many times I used to knock at his door - but that takes me back again to the importance of networking, combined with luck and a following wind. I had met Jim when he was a senior lecturer. We had previously worked on a successful project together and so he was open to my thoughts and ideas. However, I did think that although he believed in what I was saying (and never questioned my enthusiasm) he got so fed up with me knocking at his door to tell him about the benefits of learning technologies that, he eventually said: "OK Lesley, you can sit on the College IT Strategy Group". With hindsight, I now think that Jim was far more astute. Things were starting to change in the educational environment and he could genuinely see the potential for wider opportunities.

The college was at the time applying to the European Social Fund (ESF *(5)*) for a grant to explore the potential of using learning technologies to develop online management programmes. These would be developed in partnership with other EU based colleges. Even more relevant were two UK reports, both of which had a significant future impact on the use of technology-enabled learning in FE. The FEFC's *(6)* Report from the Learning Technology Committee, widely known as Higginson Report *(7)*, was completed during 1995 and published in 1996. This report ultimately led to the establishment of the National Learning Network (NLN *(8)*) and The Learning Age (1998 *(9)*), which proposed the creation of the University for Industry (Ufi *(10)*).

Being part of the college IT Strategy group was an eye opener for me. At my first meeting, I quickly realised there was a communication problem within the group around language. IT talked about server capacity, bandwidth and security issues, while management talked about funding implications and resourcing and I (with another staff representative) talked about learner benefits and staff skills. I found myself in a slightly unique position. In my career, I had previously been part of an IT support team and so I knew enough about technology and its terminology to 'hold my own' in a technical discussion, I had also worked for an organisation where bottom line business benefits had driven an IT solution, plus, I was involved with teaching and learning every day. It's only now when I reflect, I realise the key role I played was as a 'translator'.

The lessons I learned:

- *Identify potential blockers. Take time to look at the world from their perspective and engage with them on a personal level. Go and see them! Don't send emails!*
- *It's OK to work 'under the radar'. Most of the relationships you build which will reap benefits are likely to do so in both the short and longer term.*
- *Never lose sight of the bigger picture as initiatives going on outside your organisation could have a big impact on what you want to achieve.*

TWO WORLDS COLLIDE (1999)

The college secured the ESF grant to develop online distance learning management programmes. We not only needed to develop content, we also needed a platform that would host resources, track student progress and allow both tutors and students to collaborate and engage. The project manager and I spent time looking at what we wanted to achieve and what would make the programme a success. There were various Virtual Learning Environments (VLEs) available at the time all of which had very similar functionality. However one of the features we felt would be critical was collaboration between students and tutors. We therefore decided on Lotus LearningSpace, based on Lotus Notes, as it was specifically designed as a collaborative learning platform.

This led to more than a few technical issues! LearningSpace used a Domino server whilst all other college systems were Microsoft; also if you wanted to customise the 'look and feel', it had to be done in LotusScript and nobody was familiar with that language. However, the IT team agreed to support our decision and during implementation, Kirstie Coolin (on Twitter: @Kirstie_C) joined the college as the new webmaster. Kirstie was not familiar with either Domino servers or LotusScript, but she relished the challenge. I can't even begin to go into the technical issues that Kirstie overcame - maybe one day she will tell her story, but I do know she was on a very steep learning curve. Even so, within a couple of months we had a fully functional interactive and collaborative VLE.

At the beginning of 1999, I was an Associate Lecturer, which meant I was technically on a two-thirds contract. In reality, I was working full time and spending every minute I wasn't in the classroom experimenting with LearningSpace. My passion for learning had collided with my passion for technology. I was in seventh heaven! I uploaded content to support all my lessons and created workgroups and forums so that students could share their own resources and collaborate on group assignments.

Over the next few months, other lecturers were beginning to take an interest in LearningSpace. As I was a member of the IT Strategy Group, I suggested that we provide training and also that the Senior Management Team needed to actively encourage lecturers to upload resources to LearningSpace. This was approved, but it didn't quite work out as I had planned. Take-up on Continuous Professional Development (CPD) sessions was good. Lecturers attended and were interested, but that did not translate into them having 'buy in'. I really struggled to find their WIIFM. Some lecturing staff uploaded resources and activities but LearningSpace was seen more as, what we would now call, a broadcast rather than engagement mechanism. Yes, LearningSpace was being populated, but it was regarded as an online repository rather than the active collaborative environment that I hoped it would be.

Hindsight always gives us 20:20 vision. LearningSpace was not the perfect solution, but it did offer social collaboration and that was almost unheard of sixteen years ago. There were many technical issues, but technical difficulties still exist today. I found it really hard to get 'buy in' from practitioners, but yet again we are still talking about the need for 'buy in' today. However, I believe LearningSpace gave those of us involved in these very early days the opportunity to hone our skills. Those that did engage and encourage students to use LearningSpace as an additional learning resource reaped the benefits. One name that springs to mind is Dave Foord (on Twitter: @davefoord). At that time Dave was lecturing in Sports Science and he had an interest in learning technology, which he used whenever he could to support his students. Dave was a strong advocate and he pushed the boundaries. For the first time, instead of me knocking at somebody else's door I had somebody knocking at mine and that made me realise things had to change.

Although I felt I had suffered a setback, eLearning was beginning to gain momentum. In the college, we had a VLE and there were various ESF funded projects in different departments that involved producing eLearning content and resources that were not being made available on LearningSpace.... but we were working in silos, another problem that persists today.

It was time to knock on the Principal's door again. I was really struggling to drive forward the use of technology as a learning tool whilst also managing my teaching workload. Something had to give. With the support of the IT Strategy Group, I proposed a co-ordinated approach. If the college wanted to really embed eLearning, what we needed was somebody to work on this full time. It was agreed. I applied for the job and in September 1999, I was appointed as Flexible Learning Unit Co-Ordinator.

The lessons I learned:

- *Before you decide on a platform, work out what it can offer and your success criteria.*

- *You need people with both technical and learning expertise to support you.*

- *Setbacks happen. As Forest Gump said, life is "a box of chocolates" so be prepared to take the rough with the smooth.*

- *If a new role is required, fight for it and make it happen. Technology changes and, as a result, so do roles. You cannot be all things to all people all of the time, so don't spread yourself too thin.*

TIMES THEY WERE A CHANGING! (1999-2000)

Once I had a full time appointment, things moved on at a pace. Again, I have to give credit to the Loughborough College Senior Management Team as they recognised the value of learning technologies and were prepared to invest. I was, in effect, the college Information Learning Technology (ILT) Champion; a role which the following year became an NLN-funded post and was also given the remit to deliver regular CPD sessions.

My next challenge was resources. In the wider educational environment, although DVDs were slowly beginning to appear, most content was on CDROMs. The BBC released a CDROM containing short video clips of well-known sitcoms that could be used in learning. Video Arts, whose films in VHS, had long been used in FE were also made available in this format; Meetings Bloody Meetings *(11)*, featuring John Cleese, is one I remember well. To view these, students had to book copies of the discs and most had no idea that this was possible or that the content was relevant unless their lecturers told them.

We uploaded the BBC content onto the college server. This allowed staff to create links so that students could view learning-related clips from sitcoms such as 'Absolutely Fabulous' and 'The Brittas Empire' within LearningSpace. Video is great, but is only really useful in learning if the clips are short and sweet. I could tell from watching students and my children that attention span was an issue. What we needed was more very short video clips so I contacted Video Arts and asked if, provided I credited source, I could edit their videos into shorter clips. They allowed me to do this. It took a bit of time as I had to learn how to use software to edit video, but it was worth the effort. Within a short time, I was able to make lots of short video clips available to staff and student which generated more interest in eLearning.

The combination of freeing up my time as a resource to teaching staff and also that I was able to help them access useful Internet and locally stored content made a huge difference. More members of the teaching staff contacted me to find out about eLearning. This was a watershed: I could now provide them with a WIFFM. I also had the time to engage and meet with people involved in the wider community. I used to have a visit at least once a week from other FE colleges asking if they could come see what we were doing at Loughborough College.

I made contact with other organisations that had an interest in learning technologies. The FEFC, NILTA, FEDA *(12)* and Becta *(13)* were all considering the Higginson report, what it would look like in reality and how it would be implemented. The Ufi was in the final stages of deciding what their offering would be to learners. It really was an amazing and very exciting time for those of us who wanted to take learning technology forward in Further Education.

In early 2000 the Higginson report was implemented, resulting in the National Learning Network (NLN). Various organisations were given money to deliver the NLN vision and the one that was of particular interest to me was the JISC. They were tasked with setting up a network of Regional Support Centres (RSCs). Until that point, my only perception of the JISC was that they had something to do with the JANET network and that the NLN would fund colleges to get a 2MB connection to the Internet. JISC also ran mailing lists that I used to connect with like-minded people.

For me, connectivity was not particularly relevant. Loughborough College shared a campus with Loughborough University and had great connectivity. However, the RSCs role was new - it would be offering a resource to colleges in the region that went beyond far beyond connectivity. I saw this as having three aspects. Practical IT support, acting as a resource to all staff involved in learning (whether that was in teaching or in a learning resource capacity) and critical would be the support the RSC would provide to Senior Management in colleges. During my journey at Loughborough College, I knew that to achieve success you needed to ensure that you covered all three.

In our region, it was agreed that there would be a co-ordinated approach to establishing the RSC, led by the East Midlands Metropolitan Area Network (EMMAN). They arranged a meeting for all the FE Colleges and HE providers to choose lead partners. Before the meeting, I had secured the support of Loughborough University IT services team and approached our Finance Director with the question, "if I put the college's name forward as a potential host for the RSC, would the college be prepared host the RSC and provide a room big enough for five or maybe six staff?" I got an unequivocal yes!

The pre-planning paid off, it was agreed that Loughborough College and Loughborough University would be lead partners. Our submission to the Learning and Skills Council (LSC *(14)*) and the other members of the NLN was accepted. I applied for and was appointed as the RSC Manager and at that point my career which, for almost 15 years, had been classroom-focussed, changed dramatically. I understood the importance of engaging and interesting learning. I had also dipped my toes into the world of eLearning instructional design, but if I was to take learning technologies further forward and deliver the remit of the RSCs, I needed to trust the operational team I put in place and take a step back from IT support and resources. My focus needed to be on providing other colleges in the region with a solution to meet their needs and that involved staff development at all levels and strategy implementation.

The lessons I learned:

- *Never underestimate the importance of getting the SMT on board with your ideas. Once you have them on side, nurture that relationship by keeping them informed and involved.*
- *Look for partnerships beyond your organisation and recognise the importance of what you can bring to the party.*

- *Work out what the key issues will be before you enter into negotiations or meetings - and arrive prepared with a solution.*

MOVING FROM LOCAL TO REGIONAL TO NATIONAL (2000-2007)

Setting up an RSC from scratch gave me an almost blank canvas. Although there had been pilots, the model was not written in tablets of stone so we all had great flexibility in the way we structured the RSCs in our regions. From the outset, in the East Midlands, we focussed on the three areas I had identified: IT Support, support for practitioners and strategic support for senior managers.

In the short time I spent as an 'official' eLearning co-ordinator in the college, I knew how important it was to keep track of issues or problems and how they were addressed. As an RSC, we had a large client base and a team of people that would be supporting them. They had to rely on spreadsheets or memory; we needed an effective back office system. We therefore implemented a searchable Client Relationship Management (CRM) system where we could record all engagements and interactions with our user community. The system was very 'clunky' and extremely basic, but it served its purpose. As well as enabling us to build up a 'picture' of each provider, we could identify common problems and along the way develop a 'solutions bank' resulting in a better overall service. Nowadays a CRM system is commonplace, but back in 2000, we were in a whole new world and it was not something most people who worked in FE were familiar with.

I very quickly found that the issues I had identified in getting technology-enabled learning adopted in Loughborough College, were mirrored not only across the East Midlands but in all other regions as well. Without management buy-in, staff skills and internal IT support all that would be achieved would be isolated incidences where some courses would use technology to support learning whilst others wouldn't. We needed to build momentum and to do this we needed to collaborate and grow communities of practice. The RSC staff across the UK had its own community and, as part of the NLN, Becta had set up a network of ILT Champions. This was long before the days of what we now call social media, so we used JISCMail lists. In the early days, the communities that built up around these lists were invaluable but to a great extent they only involved those who were interested in and who wanted to implement technology-enabled learning.

There still had to be a WIIFM for people to change their mind-set and develop an overall strategy which would result in a change in practice. This happened for a short time in Agricultural Colleges during the 2001 foot-and-mouth outbreak *(15)*. Mobility was severely restricted so the Colleges had to very quickly find a way to provide an 'off-site' learning solution for students and technology allowed them to achieve this. Unfortunately, at the end of the outbreak, things slowly reverted back to the status quo.

In 2003, I felt I had done all I could on a regional level. The RSC was established and had made progress, but I also realised that some services would be better developed and provided at a national level. I took up a position at Becta initially as Head of Post 16 Advice and Strategy and then as Assistant Director for Institutional Development. These roles also gave me the opportunity to engage directly with the LSC and the Department for Education and Skills (DfES), giving me some (albeit limited) influence over the types of programmes offered.

I worked with an amazingly talented and very passionate team on a range of projects. These included the FERL website which provided information and advice as well as the facility for practitioners to share resources. This website was the basis of the Excellence Gateway which is currently being 'resurrected' by the Education and Training Foundation (ETF). There was also:

- The FERL Practitioners Programme, a flexible staff development framework to improve ILT skills
- A guide in the effective use of ILT for internal quality managers
- The FE Survey which gave us information about how providers were using technology-enabled learning.

We developed an E-Maturity Framework for FE, an online tool that enabled providers to self-assess their use of technology as a basis for developing an internal strategy and implementation plan. This framework was the basis for

Generator and although that is no longer available, the ETF are currently considering the development of a new on-line self-assessment tool.

This was the last FE specific project I was involved with and I have to admit, by 2007, I was becoming somewhat disillusioned. Technology was changing and the Internet in particular was changing the way people were using technology in their everyday lives. Google, Facebook, YouTube and Skype were all gaining traction. The number of eLearning vendors was growing and the quality of content was improving. Overall, the Government had spent £156m on the NLN initiative, which provided free broadband connectivity, various support projects offered by different agencies as well as a wide range of Internet based learning materials. Although there were some FE providers who embraced technology-enabled learning across the curriculum, they were in the minority. In most cases it was still only being implemented by enthusiasts.

I believe that this was, for the most part, due to the significant structural barriers that still exist in the funding and regulatory system today.

The lessons I learned:

- *A CRM can be a very effective tool and its uses extend beyond a corporate sales environment.*
- *External circumstances can have a short-term impact, but unless these continue and are supported by structural changes to the system, the status quo will prevail.*
- *Spending £m's on an initiative will not deliver the desired outcomes if the underlying regulatory structures don't support it.*

LEARNING AND DEVELOPMENT BOTH IN AND BEYOND THE WORKPLACE (2007-2014)

In 2007, Becta restructured yet again and at the same time so did Government. The DfES was split into two Departments; the Department for Children, Schools and Families (DCSF) and the Department for Universities, Innovation and Skills

(DIUS), which, in 2009, went onto become the Department for Business Innovation and Skills (BIS). My role also changed. I moved away from general FE and became Head of Regeneration and Skills where my focus was on the effective use of technology to support adult learning, both in and out of the workplace. This was a significant broadening of scope for Becta, as until then, the focus had always been on more traditional education.

The organisation that Becta contracted with to help deliver this new agenda in the corporate and third sectors was Towards Maturity *(16)*. The Towards Maturity team, headed by Laura Overton (on Twitter: @lauraoverton) supported by Head of Research, Genny Dixon provided exemplary research through their Benchmark Study *(17)*. I knew that to gain traction, we needed support from other organisations; the eLearning Network *(18)*, the organisers of the Learning Technologies Conference and Exhibition *(19)* as well as eLearning vendors and learning and development professionals. Towards Maturity rose to the challenge and assisted us in identifying the key business issues these sectors faced and the resources needed to support them. They produced a research study, Delivering Results *(20)* that contained a range of case studies to support the development of a business case for technology-enabled learning. We also produced a series of videos under the banner of Next Generation Learning @ Work; probably the best known is BT's Dare2Share *(21)* programme.

I learned a great deal between 2007 and 2011 when Becta finally closed. I met with both eLearning vendors and learning and development professionals who operate in a totally different environment to those in FE. However, I also found that in both the corporate and third sectors there were many similarities to FE. Learning and Development professionals have the same passion for learning. Those that can see the benefits of technology-enabled learning use it, but most do not. If they do, they too struggle with buy-in from senior management, have issues with IT support and in house systems blocking rather than enabling and many of their contemporaries are far more comfortable with classroom based training and creating content for classroom delivery.

In 2012, I joined the Learning and Performance Institute (LPI *(22)*) and one of the first projects I worked on was the LPI Capability Map *(23)*. The Capability Map was developed by industry experts and lists 27 skills (each with four levels of competency) required for success in the learning and development profession, including the use of technology to support learning. When taking the assessment, individuals are asked to assess themselves on those skills they think that are relevant to their current role.

Since its launch in October 2012, almost 2,000 learning professionals have carried out self-assessments. Unsurprisingly, the skills with the most assessments and the highest level of competency are face-to-face delivery (3.36) and creating content (3.13). The skills with much lower averages are those that require knowledge and understanding of technology-enabled learning, including collaborative learning (2.57) and virtual/online delivery (2.66). Whilst we may expect these figures to be lower, what is probably of greater concern is that only 48% of those who have taken the assessment believe industry awareness, which has an average score of 2.67, is part of their current role.

The lessons I learned:

- *Credibility is very important with your audience. If you don't have it, find a partner who does.*
- *Those involved in learning have many shared experiences. Don't be too quick to say, our environment is different. If you look beyond the surface, you are likely to find more similarities than differences.*

TIMES THEY ARE A CHANGING ….OR NOT?

Organisations are using technology in many different ways to engage with customers. We have seen companies that we regarded as being 'High Street Stalwarts' disappear. In many cases, this has been because they didn't embrace technology and lost sales as a result of the increase of online shopping. Online sales on Black Friday in 2014 eclipsed previous records and research is showing a big increase in purchases that we made using mobile devices. When these services are disrupted and our deliveries do not arrive on time, as consumers, we expect compensation.

Senior managers understand that customers are now demanding online services to meet their needs and yet many struggle to accept technology-enabled learning. How much competitive edge do we lose by taking this approach? Surely if employees can access learning that improves their performance and has the potential to deliver a competitive edge, this is something that senior management should not only be encouraging but nurturing?

The 'flipped classroom' is not a new concept, but how often is it used in education? There are so many excellent resources available, those produced by the Kahn Academy being an example. Using these types of resources outside the classroom, teachers and lecturers could then use time in the classroom to apply the concepts.

When I started using computers, the only way to communicate with family, friends or colleagues was either by meeting with them face to face, writing a letter or making a telephone call. And remember, as recently as the early 70s many long distance phone calls still had to be connected via the operator! The UK's phone system was not fully automatic until 1976 *(24)*. Today, provided we are connected to a network, we can communicate instantly whether we are at home, in the office or on the move. Distance is no longer a barrier, content is now device responsive and the most common complaints we hear from end users are about broadband coverage, lack of Wi-Fi and poor battery life.

Times they are a changing. We accept technology as the norm in so many areas of our lives. If we want to find out about a topic, we 'Google' it. YouTube, SlideShare, Pinterest, Quora, Wikipedia and a host of other online applications provide us with a wealth of information including learning content. Most of the changes I have seen over the last 40 years are in the advancement of technology and also in the terminology we use. In learning there are 'new' words for activities I, and many of others, have done for years. Content curation, used to be known as collating resources. One of the main reasons I implemented LearningSpace as a VLE in 1998 was the platform. It was specifically designed for sharing content and allowing comments within groups, but didn't call it social and collaborative learning. I used

WebQuests which set learners online challenges but didn't even think of calling it gamification.

The question I keep coming back to is this: why we are not making more effective use of technology to support both formal and informal learning in education and in the workplace? There are so many more options available now than there were twenty years ago. In education there are still regulatory and funding changes to be made, however, are we using these as a reason or excuse for maintaining the status quo? There are not the same restrictions in workplace learning. Progress is being made, but it is not moving as fast as the changes in technology. As Learning Professionals, we should be viewing these changes as an opportunity not a threat and when we do that then we will be in a position to say times really are a changing.

So, in conclusion, here are the key lessons I have learned over the years:

- *Technology doesn't stand still, embrace it. Organisations that have not done so, no longer exist.*
- *Take responsibility for your own personal development and be industry-aware. To achieve this, you need to look beyond learning and the environment you work in.*
- *Build personal networks and relationships that are based on trust. They take time, energy and effort to maintain, but the benefits are immeasurable.*

NOTES

1. Where in the World is Carmen Sandiego: http://en.wikipedia.org/wiki/Where_in_the_World_Is_Carmen_Sandiego%3F

2. National Information Learning Technology Association: http://en.wikipedia.org/wiki/AoC_NILTA

3. WebQuest: http://en.wikipedia.org/wiki/WebQuest

4. InfoTrac: http://en.wikipedia.org/wiki/InfoTrac

5. ESF: http://en.wikipedia.org/wiki/European_Social_Fund

6. FEFC: http://en.wikipedia.org/wiki/Further_Education_Funding_Council_for_England

7. Higginson Report: http://iltinfe.files.wordpress.com/2011/04/000255_report_of_the_learning_and_technology_committee_-_higginson.pdf

8. NLN: http://en.wikipedia.org/wiki/National_Learning_Network

9. The Learning Age: http://www.lifelonglearning.co.uk/greenpaper/

10. Ufi: http://en.wikipedia.org/wiki/Learndirect

11. Meetings Bloody Meetings: https://www.youtube.com/watch?v=ZWYnVt-umSA

12. FEDA: http://en.wikipedia.org/wiki/Learning_and_Skills_Development_Agency

13. Becta: http://en.wikipedia.org/wiki/Becta

14. LSC: http://en.wikipedia.org/wiki/Learning_and_Skills_Council

15. 2001 Foot and Mouth outbreak: http://en.wikipedia.org/wiki/2001_United_Kingdom_foot-and-mouth_outbreak

16. Toward Maturity: http://www.towardsmaturity.org/

17. Benchmark Study: http://towardsmaturity.org/article/2014/11/05/modernising-learning-delivering-results-2014/

18. eLearning Network: http://www.elearningnetwork.org/

19. Learning Technologies Conference and Exhibition: http://www.learningtechnologies.co.uk/page.cfm?Action=Visitor/VisitorID=92/loadSearch=11924_2756

20. Delivering Results: http://www.towardsmaturity.org/article/2010/02/17/delivering-results-learning-technology-workplace-n/

21. BT – Dare2Share Project: https://www.youtube.com/watch?v=gtVYkEdGtfo

22. LPI: https://www.learningandperformanceinstitute.com/

23. LPI Capability Map: https://www.learningandperformanceinstitute.com/capabilitymap.htm

24. STD Dialing Fully Automatic: http://news.bbc.co.uk/onthisday/hi/dates/stories/september/5/newsid_3070000/3070819.stm

CITATION

Price, L. (2015). Times they are a changing .. or not?. In: Hopkins, D., ed., The Really Useful #EdTechBook, 1st ed. David Hopkins, pp.107-128.

THE BLENDED PROFESSIONAL: JACK-OF-ALL-TRADES AND MASTER OF SOME?

SUE BECKINGHAM

Educational Developer and Lecturer, Sheffield Hallam University

@suebecks

http://socialmediaforlearning.com/

Sue is an Educational Developer and Lecturer at Sheffield Hallam University and takes a lead role in her faculty for Technology Enhanced Learning. Her research interests include the use of social media in higher education, online identity and digital literacies. Sue writes a blog on the use of social media.

Within the last decade we have experienced an unprecedented growth in the use of technology in education. The adoption of Virtual Learning Environments (VLEs) for many universities has been widespread. Granted the speed of which this has been integrated is influenced by local policy, the academics themselves and the support available to learn how to use the VLE and its suite of tools. However, there has been a shift from just having a small central eLearning team who reached out to encourage staff to use the VLE, to a growing need for a wider pool of people to support colleagues who want to learn why and how technology can be used to enhance their teaching practice. Today the VLE is just one aspect; mobile learning and educational Apps, social media, and webinars are just some of the many examples being used to develop communication, collaboration and social learning. Some institutions (or indeed faculties within them) have looked to create roles for Learning Technologists to support such development, and yet others have relied on the early adopters and enthusiasts to assume this role. This chapter will look at some short case studies and reflections of the 'blended professionals' who are advocates of #EdTech and how the need to wear different hats to meet very different objectives can present surprising results when supported within a community of practice.

INTRODUCTION

In this chapter I am going to begin by sharing with you my personal account of what it means to be a blended professional and the wearer of multiple hats. When I moved into my role ten years ago as an Educational Developer, technology was not in the job description. However as time moved on it was clear to me that there were many new ways we could look to enhance the way we approached learning and teaching. I consider myself as an early adopter in the use of educational technology and have explored this for my own benefit as a lifelong and lifewide learner as well as helping others to do so. However I am hesitant to say that I am a Learning Technologist and will explain why. I will also share some mini case studies of other colleagues who have become EdTech champions within their own roles. Finally I will guide you through some approaches to consider as a blended educator and advocate of the use of technology in education.

WHAT IS A BLENDED PROFESSIONAL

Being a blended professional for me is where an individual takes on a variety of different roles. These hybrid roles often overlap and can provide the individual with a growing knowledge of multiple areas. The ability to absorb and understand information from different perspectives is key, as is the ability to be 'multilingual' and communicate in a variety of ways and to different audiences. Whitchurch (2008) describes the blended profession as those "*not only crossing internal and external institutional boundaries, but also contributing to the development of new forms of third space between professional and academic domains*". To add the individual can take on hybrid responsibilities resulting in the need to be both multi-skilled and working within and across multifunctional teams. The development of inter- and intra-team communication is also important and they may work within and with a number of different teams. A hybrid professional often needs to undertake new CPD to develop skills in the additional areas of responsibility as they emerge.

MY PERSONAL CASE STUDY

The role I applied for doesn't formally have technology in the job description. I assumed responsibility for eLearning over the course of time because of my interest in educational technology and how, if used well it can enhance the learning experience both for the student and the academic seeking to undertake professional development. This interest, which has developed into a passion for exploring new innovative ways to manage my own learning as well as to help others, has developed through undertaking a broad range of CPD myself.

If I had to pinpoint when my interest in educational technology was first piqued, I think it would be as a result of my somewhat uncomfortable experience as a distance learning (DL) student on a short course. The feeling of isolation and loneliness was a stark contrast to the one I was experiencing for the classroom-based Masters course I was taking concurrently. At the same time my daughter had just gone away to start her undergraduate degree and, through texts and social media (plus the odd phone call), we exchanged experiences, provided moral support and, to some extent, I was able to mentor her and help her navigate the swamp of academic 'speak and protocols'. Both our experiences were enhanced by the use of technology as we developed our new peer networks. This use of digital tech we refer to as social media or social networking, provided the mechanism to extend the conversations within the classroom to outside of, and this also became a place to socialise and feel part of a community. What was missing from the DL course I was taking was the opportunity for students to socialise and get to know each other. Yes there was a Moodle discussion forum but (for me) it never seemed to be used to build a sense of community. It felt like a billboard to post your mini bio or CV.

During the research I undertook for my first Masters thesis in 2009, I looked initially at computer-mediated technology with a particular interest in how texting was being used. As I started to look more deeply at the use and appropriation of social media, I realised there were many new ways being adopted to enhance the way we communicate. This then led to how it could impact on the learning experience and learning journey of both me and my daughter, and also my peers. What was also interesting was that educators were starting to openly share how they were using social media and other technology through social media channels. What they shared was much richer than simply what they were doing, but also why, how and what the impact was. At this point I was hooked! The realisation that I had at my fingertips the most incredible learning network was to me phenomenal. Not only could I read and learn from these golden nuggets shared by this community, I had the opportunity to raise questions and in time answer those raised by others.

TAKING ON AN EDTECH ROLE

In 2008 I was given the opportunity to recruit and line manage a placement student who would take on the role of eLearning Assistant and work with me within one Faculty to engage academic staff with Blackboard. A new policy was introduced where every module should be supported by a Blackboard site. This to some degree was quite a steep learning curve for both of us as within this same year the university upgraded the VLE from Blackboard 8 to 9.1. For those of you familiar with such a step you will know that this is not simply the IT team doing techy stuff in the background! The new version meant that all staff needed to be updated on the changes and this required us to work with the eLearning teams across the university to roll out training sessions to maximise reach; to create new written resources and provide different ways to communicate with staff why it was important to engage with this in readiness for the new academic year; and to be there to provide at elbow support as academics began to use the new version.

As I began to grasp the various aspects of this new dimension to my role I realised I had to learn on the hoof. Drawing upon the expertise of other eLearning teams across the university and of the central Technology Enhanced Learning (TEL) team was a crucial and incredibly supportive. Shadowing peers as they ran workshops is possibly one of the most useful ways to getting started. Having an online network to reach out to and ask questions or table ideas is also key. However, as this was just part of my responsibilities, there was a concern that I wasn't able to devote time to grasp a deeper practical understanding of the multiple functionalities of the VLE. However my eLearning Assistant could. It took me a while to accept that as a Manager I did not have to know everything.

Fast forward to 2014 and EdTech is now so much broader than the VLE. The affordances of technology present us with a myriad of shiny tools and Apps that can and are being used. A growing interest in the use of social media, mobile and smart technology, Apps and software has piqued curiosity from others and as a consequence an increased demand for support. The growth in the sharing of open educational resources and EdTech has in itself opened a floodgate of exciting innovative practice. This for many has contributed to the increased interest and also presented a forum for support. It certainly has for me.

BLENDING TECHNOLOGY INTO MY BLENDED PROFESSIONAL ROLES

During a typical working week my blended role includes being:

- An educational developer
- A lecturer
- A researcher
- An eLearning or TEL faculty lead
- A manager
- A Learning, Teaching and Assessment (LTA) coordinator
- A student

For each of these roles I may work with different individuals and groups of people. The one common theme is that for both myself and others with a blend of any of these roles, we all engage to some extent with learning and teaching in higher education. Having multiple roles can often mean that we are required to consider decisions from a variety of different angles and perspectives. Equally the way we approach using technology may differ, but can also overlap.

As an Educational Developer and Fellow of the Staff and Educational Development Association (SEDA) I work with others within higher education to provide academic staff with educational and professional development. This could be one to one very individual support, advice on curriculum development, or to support the implementation of change and new policies. I am committed to putting into practice the SEDA values which are:

- Developing an understanding of how people learn

- Practising in ways that are scholarly, professional and ethical
- Working with and developing learning communities
- Valuing diversity and promoting inclusivity
- Continually reflecting on practice to develop ourselves, others and processes.

Within this role I not only work with colleagues within my own university but with Educational Developers across the UK. Digital collaboration using, for example, Google Apps, has been a very useful application of technology and broken down geographical boundaries through the use of Google Hangouts and Skype.

As a *lecturer* I look to adopt new ways to enhance the way I teach and engage learners, but also in the way I introduce assessment for learning and feedback of learning. Technology has played a part in this and provided variety in the way this is approached. Integrating the opportunities for my students to develop valuable digital skills is a key focus.

As a *researcher* I am striving to explore, understand, evaluate and share how technology can enhance learning. More often than not this is done outside of my day to day responsibilities, but is an area I feel very passionate about. From my own personal perspective, the use of technology has helped me to organise my own learning.

As a *TEL lead* I have faculty objectives to meet and as a manager of my small team, a responsibility to ensure that together we achieve these, but also that my eLearning Assistant is supported in his role and developed with the skills to do his job. Together we are using technology to create resources to support the use of technology, for example screencasts as how to guides.

As an *LTA coordinator* I am responsible for delivering a variety of workshops to enhance and develop the curriculum and the LTA orientation of new academics; leading the organisation of the annual faculty LTA conference; am a member of a variety of committees including the HEA Recognition Panel; and am the coordinator of teaching enhancement projects. Using technology to communicate and disseminate this work is enhanced through the updating of the LTA website and blog, utilising multimedia where appropriate.

As a *student* I have gone on to take a second Masters degree in Technology Enhanced Learning, Innovation and Change, to better my understanding of how to inspire innovation and overcome barriers to change. As I have referred to earlier this has been a most inspiring and innovative sandpit and learning space. I have gone on to apply much of what I have learned across my various roles.

So you can see that learning technology is associated and ingrained within each of my different roles, through the examples given above. However because EdTech is not 100% of my focus due to having mixed responsibilities I have never thought of myself as a Learning Technologist. Yet when you look at the definition of this role I am contributing to and actively involved in each of the areas mentioned.

> *Learning technologists are people who are actively involved in managing, researching, supporting or enabling learning with the use of learning technology. (ALT 2014)*

In many higher education institutions there are people with a Learning Technologist role, where the individual has a dedicated role relating to the use of technology and learning. Learning technology (ALT 2014) is the "*broad range of communication, information and related technologies that can be used to support learning, teaching, and assessment.*" I know many Learning Technologists across a variety of universities and personally look to them for their deep understanding of both the technical use of technology but also the pedagogical application and evaluation of a broad range of learning technology. Indeed many are authors within this book! My skills do not match theirs in the sense of scope, however I do specialise in some areas.

Am I therefore perhaps a 'Jack of all trades and master of some'? Perhaps, but I would forward the suggestion that I am an educational innovator and that through the use of EdTech I am making positive steps and enhancing the way I learn and teach others. I am also not alone. Having had a number of conversations with colleagues in my valued personal learning network that might be considered blended professionals, I feel their stories should be heard too.

MINI CASE STUDIES OF OTHER ED TECH BLENDED PROFESSIONALS

Below I have chosen five colleagues from my own university, each with different roles, but all sharing the concept of being a blended professional to some extent. They all share an interest in EdTech and this has become implicit in the way they work. These are individuals who have never had EdTech written in to their job description but are individuals who seek to innovate their own practice, but also go on to inspire and mentor peers within their own community to do so too. These are not just early adopters, but digital champions.

Julie Gillin - Journalist Lecturer

"As a journalism lecturer I'd witnessed technological advances which had brought incredible disruption and change to journalism practice. Like many of my colleagues, I'd spent a lot of time working to keep my own skills up-to-date and to ensure these changes were reflected in our curriculum. However, I became increasingly aware that while my discipline was being transformed, the way I was teaching wasn't. I was interested in the way technology could improve my teaching but I was also somewhat overwhelmed by the possibilities and by a concern that I wasn't as digitally literate a lecturer as I'd like to be. It was this which led me to join the TELIC (Technology Enhanced Learning, Innovation and Change) course at Sheffield Hallam University.

"Joining the course had an incredible impact on my teaching and on my own CPD which, I have to be honest, had lacked focus. The biggest change was the development of my own PLN which began with working collaboratively with fellow students. Supported by our tutors and each other we used technology in our learning. Sometimes it went wrong! Realising that this happens to everyone and is not a reflection on you and doesn't mean you are somehow inadequate was incredibly liberating. Right from the first few months of my TELIC course I found I had the

confidence to introduce technology into my teaching. At first this was often using tools or apps we had used on the course as I felt comfortable using them but gradually, as my PLN developed mainly through social media, I discovered new tools and, more importantly, if I found something I wanted to achieve in my seminars I looked for tools to do it, rather than the other way around. I don't think of myself as particularly 'techie' and there is sometimes the odd glitch but I'm confident about trying different things and I know if I'm struggling I've a network to lean on to help me out just as I'm keen to help others. As a result, I've a whole new range of teaching and learning tools which allow me to adapt to the different students and topics I come across. I've stopped thinking about this being 'new' or 'different' but rather technology enhanced teaching and learning is just what I do, it has become a natural part of my teaching and learning."

Julie has been a mentor to many of her peers within her team and beyond and certainly inspires me with her innovative ideas.

Claire Ridall - Learning and Information Systems Portfolio Manager, Learning Centre

"The library was invited to act as a client with a cohort of students from a level 5 module in ACES to develops a two minute animation showing the benefits of using the libraries. During the first session, it transpired that over 50% of the group had not used the library before other than to access resources online through the library gateway. The best advocate of library services and resources would ideally be the student voice, and two fully developed animations by chosen students were commissioned to create shareable content that showcased the library offer in an entertaining and accessible format. One student delivered an animation in an interview setting, with a journalist asking questions of the main protagonist, 'Giles'. The student chose to portray all characters apart from the interviewer as different organs of the human body to ensure there was no prejudice or discrimination against gender or race, and to avoid stereotyping the concept of students.

137

"Both of the final versions of the animations were presented to library staff at an away day, to University senior staff from academic departments as a way of showcasing student talent and as a reflection of the library's offer to students and the value that it holds in the student journey. The videos were added to online YouTube channels, promoted on Twitter to students and staff, played in induction sessions and played on corporate plasma television screens on-campus. Feedback from students was resoundingly positive to the point where further animations on different library facilities are being developed by more students, and awareness of the library offer through conversations on Twitter and in demand and usage across the library services and facilities."

Claire makes effective use of social media to share the many resources and events from the Learning Centre and personally through her own Twitter account, consistently sharing useful information with her personal learning network. She works with a team who co-write the Library blog and Twitter, which is managed using Sprout Social as it's a useful tool to plot engagement and audience demographics.

David Eddy -Teaching Fellow for Distance Learning

"EdTech has played an increasing role in my teaching over recent years and is now absolutely integral in a context where this is all undertaken via online distance learning. Whilst pedagogical approach and learning design are the foremost drivers, EdTech offers a number of affordances in terms of access and the utilisation of synchronous and asynchronous communication, which has enhanced my practice. These affordances also extend to the documentation and recording of CPD evidence and reflection on my practice via e portfolio, digital profiles, peer review and professional accreditation. EdTech affordances have allowed me to develop a digital voice and more readily collaborate, share, present and showcase work I have undertaken."

To add David has utilised a wide range of EdTech in his teaching and has inspired those within and beyond his peers by openly sharing and talking about his work. He is a regular user of Twitter and uses this forum to interact with educators across the globe.

Professor Mike Bramhall - Assistant Dean Academic Development

Mike in his senior role continues to teach and has been a keen advocate of the use of video with students utilising video cameras, flip cameras, and more recently iPads and mobile phones. Digital video reporting was introduced to replace the more traditional written report and oral PowerPoint presentation for students in Materials Engineering. The main identified outcomes were:

- Increased student motivation
- Enhanced learning experience
- Higher marks
- Development potential for deeper learning of the subject
- Development of learner autonomy
- Enhanced team working and communication skills
- A source of evidence relating to skills for interviews 4
- Learning resources for future cohorts to use
- Opportunities for staff development (CPD).

Mike told me his decision to innovate the way he was teaching was down to him valuing the use of technology to aid student creativity and enabling opportunities for his students to do something different from the norm to make it more fun and interesting.

Professor Roger Eccleston - Pro Vice Chancellor, Faculty of Arts Computing Engineering and Sciences

My final colleague is Dean of the Faculty I work within, and he holds an overarching role that spans teaching, research, technical and professional services. His use of technology has seen him become a role model for others in the use of social media and multimedia as a communication channel to share the work of students and staff across the faculty. For so many this has been welcomed as a visual acknowledgement of their work. It has also encouraged others to start to use Twitter and develop a LinkedIn profile.

Such case studies are important to share so that others can see a broader range of activities that extend beyond the traditional classroom and impact on the wider student experience. It can also serve to demonstrate that those engaging with innovative EdTech are not techy people. Curiosity, enthusiasm and willingness to try something new are what is needed and my colleagues certainly demonstrate this!

CONFESSIONS OF AN EDUCATIONAL INNOVATOR

I'm not a tech expert by any means, however I do consider myself as an early adopter of technology, an educational innovator and someone that is willing to dive in and try new things. In particular technology that can enhance the way we can connect with others to communicate and collaborate. As a student on the MSc in Technology Enhanced Learning Innovation and Change at Sheffield Hallam University we (myself and my peers) were positively encouraged to explore and experiment with new technology, Apps and approaches to the way we were learning. As a cohort we created our own support network and Julie Gillen and Phil Vincent played a significant part in this for me. Where one got stuck, there was always someone to reach out to. This was a distance learning course so we learnt quickly how to make good use of Google Hangouts and other collaborative tools. My experience has gone on to influence the way I consider the use of technology in all aspects of my role.

I recently read a book called the Six Thinking Hats (de Bono 1985). As I was reading I thought it would actually be useful to consider de Bono's six different approaches to thinking in relation to my own role, given the many hats I seem to wear. As I go on to explain what these are, you will begin to understand why it is important for me (and you may also resonate with this), to take off my favoured green thinking hat and consider the other five, but also to give the people I work with the opportunity to do so too.

Let me introduce you to de Bono (1985) who reminds us of the value of thinking and how we should use this to open our minds, but also how we can 'focus in' by considering things from different angles. He presents six thinking styles, which are colour coded, and each signifies a different perspective (1985:13). The colours he uses are white, red, black, yellow, green and blue. These are explained as follows:

WHITE HAT THINKING	RED HAT THINKING
• White is neutral and objective. • The white hat is concerned with objective facts and figures. • White Hat thinking focuses on data, facts, information known or needed.	• Red suggests anger (seeing red), rage and emotions. • The red hat gives the emotional view • Red Hat thinking focuses on feelings, hunches, gut instinct, and intuition.
BLACK HAT THINKING	YELLOW HAT THINKING
• Black is sombre and serious. • The black hat is cautious and careful. It points out the weaknesses in an idea. • Black Hat thinking focuses on difficulties, potential problems. Why something may not work.	• Yellow is sunny and positive. • The yellow hat is optimistic and covers hope and positive thinking. • Yellow Hat thinking focuses on values and benefits. Why something may work.
GREEN HAT THINKING	BLUE HAT THINKING
• Green is grass, vegetation and abundant, fertile growth. • The green hat indicated creativity and new ideas. • Green Hat thinking focuses on creativity: possibilities, alternatives, solutions, new ideas.	• Blue is cool, and it is also the colour of the sky, which is above everything else. • The blue hat is concerned with control, the organisation of the thinking process and the use of the other hats. • Blue Hat thinking focuses on managing the thinking process, focus, next steps, action plans.

(de Bono 1985)

Well, as I confessed, I am frequently the wearer of the green hat. Green hat thinking focuses on creativity; possibilities, alternatives, solutions, new ideas. I can quite cheerfully identify a new technology and jump in to try it out and consider how this might be used as a new creative approach to learning and teaching. I am however equally happy to share the failures as well as the successes and I try to present a balanced view holding my hand up when things don't work so well and sharing why this is so. Whilst this is fine for my own teaching I am also aware that creative thinking and ideas can be for some a little daunting or considered risky. Through my enthusiasm I have to take care I don't get carried away at times.

I have found using de Bono's different thinking styles a useful exercise. It can be done either individually or as a team to consider the way you approach the work you undertake. I will now share with you how I have considered the different thinking styles in relation to different aspects of my multiple roles, why I feel that each is important, and how acknowledging and providing space for different thinking styles can be of great value.

White Hat thinking focuses on data, facts, information known or needed.

In my role I need to consider the annual TEL objectives I have been set and how together with my colleague how we plan to achieve these. An example would be to introduce online assessment and feedback across the faculty. de Bono (1985: 25) suggests our starting point has to be:

- What information do we have?
- What information do we need?
- What information is missing?
- What questions do we need to ask?
- How are we going to get the information we need?

Considerations might be how many are already using online assessment and feedback, how many need training and support to consider using technology for this purpose, how will this data be collected.

Red Hat thinking focuses on feelings, hunches, gut instinct, and intuition.

Here I need to consider my feelings towards the

implementation of educational technology, but more importantly I need to give the staff I am working with the opportunity to voice their feelings. Each individual may have a different reaction. It is important to acknowledge this and not pass judgment. Where colleagues are perhaps resistant to using technology, it is helpful to provide exemplars where possible of where it has been used in their subject or discipline area. Giving the person I am working with the time to explain their concerns could reveal a fear of the technology, a concern about the time it will take to implement, or unclarity about how it could enhance the student experience. Talking through such issues will allow me to offer support of at-elbow training, show how their time can be saved and how it can be of value to the students they are teaching.

Black Hat thinking *focuses on difficulties, potential problems.*

Why something may not work. This is where I need to consider issues raised by the individuals or groups of academics I work with. There are going to be occasions where they are critical of a suggested approach. Where there are weaknesses and potential problems identified, these can and should be discussed. It is important to give the space and time to get beyond the just critical comments such as "*this will never work in our subject area*". It may be the individual is just being cautious. Sharing experiences with peers in similar roles is also very useful as one, it can identify a common issue for all or two, it can provide useful exemplars where issues have been overcome.

Yellow Hat thinking *focuses on values and benefits. Why something may work.*

Now this is where there is an opportunity to get others to rethink and consider previously dismissed innovations. Working with an optimist can encourage others within the group to explore the new innovation presented. Focussing on the benefits such as saving time on writing feedback by introducing an online marking

143

rubric or introducing an online assessment submission area so that students can do this from wherever they are can be positively received. De Bono (1985: 94) suggests that 'self-interest is a strong basis for positive thinking' so using this as a starting place for discussion is helpful. This can then lead into sharing scenarios and exemplars of practice; then a discussion on what went well, why it was effective and how do you know.

Green Hat thinking *focuses on creativity: possibilities, alternatives, solutions, new ideas.*

Another approach when working with a group is to ask individuals to share their ideas. This is space to consider new options and different approaches. Going with 'all ideas are good ideas', these can be gathered and then reviewed. This might start with how a learning activity is currently being approached and what the concerns are. Thinking creatively gives them permission to look at perhaps doing a task in an easier way or approaching it in a different way. So for example students are not collecting their assignments with the attached feedback as they already retrieved their mark online. Exploring whether online feedback is accessed more is one measure but experimenting with different types of feedback and then getting feedback from the students could reveal that written feedback with no opportunity to question it is unhelpful.

Blue Hat thinking *focuses on managing the thinking process, focus, next steps, action plans.*

In the context of my work this might represent my conscience. Have I given due consideration to the different approaches to thinking and have I given others the opportunity to do so too. I might want to consider if I have understood a problem presented by a colleague and whether I have asked the right questions before coming up with a plan of action.

OVERCOMING OBSTACLES

For some the use of technology is still seen as unnecessary, a threat or an inconvenience. Why change when we have always done it like this?

Henry Ford is famously quoted as saying "*If I'd asked people what they wanted, they would have said faster horses*". Instead he developed a motor car that they could afford. This was initially only available in one colour - black. Of course today we know that not only can we choose different colours for cars, we have a vast and varied choice of models and specifications. We have embraced these changes and see the choices as positive enhancements. How can we adopt this mindset in relation to innovating teaching with technology? From my experience this begins with starting with basics. Give too many choices and options and the very person you are trying to help can become overwhelmed.

STRIKING A BALANCE

Keeping up with the growing array of educational technology is no small task. I am often reminded that we cannot in our roles as EdTech educators support every technology there is. Yet there is a tension that where the technologies are determined as a list our very creativity can be stifled. Once you see the value of technology you want to try out new approaches. Time can be a concern, but my innovative journeys of exploration are often done in my own time and tested by me in my role as a lifewide learner.

In companies such as Google and LinkedIn employees have dedicated innovation time. Hack-athons are frequently seen to bring people together to work on a time limited project. Developing the developer (Cowan 1998) is an important aspect to consider and more so where you undertake a blended role and don't work within a team focusing on technology. If we are all to become users of technology to enhance learning and teaching, then perhaps it is now time to review the support needed for such development to take place. There are now different ways we can approach this and not all have to be face to face. Webinars and screencasts using free tools such as Google Hangouts, Skype, YouTube, Vimeo and Screencast-o-matic are excellent ways to introduce initial tutorials that can complement face to face sessions. Organised workshops need to be planned in advance so that these can be communicated and interested attendees can find space in busy diaries. Planning group co-learning sessions are often well received.

Wojkicki (2011) and Google's Eight Pillars of Innovation provide a useful framework to work within. I have used this to present some examples of the steps I have taken, in the hope that this can demonstrate that like many others we all had to start somewhere. Using technology to innovate learning begins with you. Playing and experimenting with technology is a vital step in building your own confidence.

Wojkicki (2011) and Google's Eight Pillars of Innovation provide a useful framework to work within (see Figure 1):

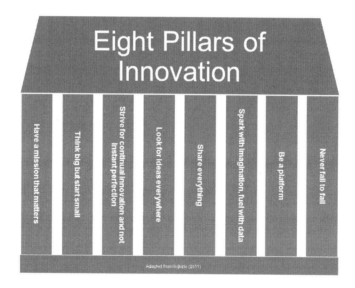

Figure 1. Wojkicki (2011) adaption of Google's Eight Pillars of Innovation

1. Have a mission that matters

Consider what you want to achieve. Helping others realise the value of a professional online presence (educators and students) is one example I wanted to achieve.

2.   Think big but start small

Starting a blog using WordPress was the platform I chose to use, to write about online presence and the role of social media. It was free and easy to use.

3.   Strive for continual innovation and not instant perfection

Adding screencasts to provide a voice over for PowerPoint presentations can add value to a post - speaking naturally means that there might be the odd 'erms' and 'ums' but it doesn't detract from what you are saying. It really does not have to be polished and perfect.

4.   Look for ideas everywhere

Twitter is possibly the richest space for finding useful information, primarily as these short posts can link to a wide variety of sources that include books, articles, journals, videos, blog posts, lesson plans, debates and more.

5.   Share everything

As I developed information about the topic of professional online presence (and others) I wrote blog posts and added presentations to SlideShare - these were then shared via Twitter, added to LinkedIn and Google+. I give my work a Creative Commons licence. I also share the work of others through the same forums.

6.   Spark with imagination, fuel with data

Using images in posts and tweets catches the eye. Numbers also speak volumes and can be shared visually as infographics and digital posters. Express information in different and creative ways by utilising the many free tools that are now available to us.

7.   Be a platform

Find an area of interest and gather information. Start with a private blog tagging useful resources. Go on to share this information through the digital forum of your choice. Share with others where this is and provide links to interconnect your profiles.

8.   Never fail to fail

It is how we learn. If something goes wrong, don't worry. There is always someone to ask and increasingly this is done online through help forums, Twitter and via comments on blogs.

SOME FINAL THOUGHTS

Two decades ago Cowan (1998:123) gave the following advice on becoming an innovative university teacher and how to get started. His following list of bulleted points is equally applicable for the Learning Technologist and the Educational Developer. They are now pinned to the wall of my office as a reminder.

When introducing innovation of any kind but especially technology, keep a log of what your intended outcomes are, the steps taken to introduce the innovation and collate feedback from students and peers along the way. This informal diary can be invaluable to reflect upon and serve as notes to help you decide on future interventions. Evaluating what we do differently is possibly the one area we are not always so good at completing or indeed sharing, and yet in doing so we can all benefit and learn together going forward.

Innovative Teaching (Cowan 1998):
- Taking risks
- Iterating
- In any pilot, entering into a partnership with the students concerned
- The almost evangelical impact of some innovatory personalities
- Basing what you attempt on your beliefs about what matters in learning, and for learners
- Watching out for mismatches, and reacting positively to them
- Turning mistakes into positive lessons learned
- Benefiting from reflecting on teaching, as much as getting learners to benefit from reflecting about learning
- Using inputs from those with experience, once a first declaration of interest has been made
- Experiencing teaching and learning situations as a learner, especially when these are unfamiliar or novel

- Publishing accounts of innovation
- Repeating previous research or development studies, in your own field
- Formative evaluations verging on action-research, with students joining in interpreting the lessons to be learned for development
- Partnership with kindred spirits who are not necessarily experts in the field, which lead on to valuable cooperation
- Cross-disciplinary transfer of ideas and contacts
- Experimentation off one's own territory, where it is easier to recover from failure
- Being almost Machiavellian in the activity outlines you devise, in order to achieve certain learning outcomes or even win space to attempt them
- Being tactical in relations with colleagues and institutions
- Making provision to develop the developer, in all of this
- Being prepared to get it wrong.

REFERENCES

ALT (2014) Association for Learning Technology. https://www.alt.ac.uk/

de Bono, E. (1985) Six Thinking Hats. London: Penguin Books.

Cowan, J. (1998) On Becoming an Innovative University Teacher. Buckingham: SRHE and Open University Press.

SEDA (2014) The Staff and Educational Development Association. https://seda.ac.uk

Whitchurch, C. (2008). Shifting Identities and Blurring Boundaries: the Emergence of Third Space Professionals in UK Higher Education. Higher Education Quarterly, 62(4), pp. 377-396. Available at: http://dx.doi.org/10.1111/j.1468-2273.2008.00387.x

Whitchurch, C. (2009) The rise of the blended professional in higher education: a comparison between the United Kingdom, Australia and the United States. Higher Education, 58(3), pp. 407-418. Available at: http://link.springer.com/article/10.1007/s10734-009-9202-4

Wojkicki, S. (2011) The Eight Pillars of Innovation. [Online] Available at:

https://ssl.gstatic.com/think/docs/8-pillars-of-innovation_articles.pdf

CITATION

Beckingham, S. (2015). The blended professional: Jack of all trades, and master of some?. In: Hopkins, D., ed., *The Really Useful #EdTechBook*, 1st ed. David Hopkins, pp.129-150.

HOW GADGETS HELP US LEARN

JULIAN STODD

Author, Founder of SeaSalt Learning

@julianstodd

http://julianstodd.wordpress.com/

Technology surrounds us, changes us, but how do we actually use it to learn? I'm proposing to explore different aspects of technology as it relates to learning in the Social Age. Specifically:

- **Community**: the function of our social communities and the ways in which the technology connects us to them and each other. Includes exploring the role we take and the purpose they serve in social learning methodologies
- **Storytelling**: the ways that form and share authentic stories to communicate
- **Reputation** and social authority: exploring social reputation and how it is facilitated by technology
- **Measurement**: looking at how the quantified self meets the qualified self.

My underlying premise is that great learning (be it mobile, face to face, eLearning or social) needs to be designed to create spaces for 'context', 'demonstration', 'exploration', 'reflection', 'assessment' and 'performance support'. The technology itself can facilitate this, in some areas more than others, but is only facilitating: it doesn't guarantee the quality and effectiveness if the design is wrong.

INTRODUCTION

We live in the Social Age, a time of constant change, a time when technology connects and empowers us, helps us to be better. Helps us to learn and work, helps us to drive change. The day of the dinosaurs is over: it is no longer about one system, one technology and one way of doing things: the Social Age is typified by multiple communities serving multiple purposes, by different technologies and systems that are interconnected yet independent.

It is about agility: about sense making within communities and doing things differently tomorrow. It is not about learning once and doing many times, but rather about information when we need it and communities to help make sense of it. The Social Age is about uninhibited curiosity, about equality and fairness, the amplification of ideas and the democratisation of communication.

Which is all very well, but what does it actually mean and how does technology actually help us to learn?

In this chapter, we will be exploring different facets of technology and reflecting upon how the gadgets actually help us to be better.

THE ECOSYSTEM OF THE SOCIAL AGE

Things aren't what they used to be. My grandmother used to talk about how, when she was young, people still used horses and carriages to travel. That's one long stretch from horses to Skype in less than a hundred years. We have seen evolutions in transport and technology, social habits and politics. A pace of change that is increasing; each change unlocks permission for more change.

Take work: we used to leave school, get a degree, find a graduate position and start our way up the ladder. Except suddenly the ladder got a whole lot more rickety. People started to lose their jobs and there was a certain stigma attached to it: redundancy was a badge of shame for some. Except it kept coming, it happened to more people as the market became less stable. Suddenly you were in a minority if you hadn't lost a job somewhere along the way. The organisations we work for became more susceptible to the ebb and flow of the tides and less able to weather the change without changing themselves.

'Human Resources' and 'Capital' were the names that charted our descent into mere collateral, merely pawns to be deployed and sacrificed at will.

And yet the equation was not balanced: still demands were made of us to give more, to work harder, to support change and commit our hearts and souls.

At first, we were given open plan offices and expected to like them. Then telephones and laptops: badges of honour and success. We were rewarded with environment and infrastructure, given technology to keep us passive, that passivity enforced through IT policies and, latterly, social media ones. Mechanisms of control that we were expected to be grateful for. Like giving a carpenter a saw and expecting them to be grateful for the chance to hold it.

But something happened: the social contract started to fracture. When we had job security and a career path, we were willing to trade freedom for technology, infrastructure and a pay cheque. But when the security went, and as the technology started to liberalise, the balance moved out of our favour.

Suddenly, the computers and laptops that we had once prized started to feel a bit clunky: the black plastic feeling decidedly corporate as it invaded our homes and pockets. Suddenly we had options, and those options were white, silver, sleek, fun and, crucially, ours to own and control.

For a while, the two co-existed: people had 'social' technology and 'formal'. We started carrying two phones in our pockets, a work and a play one. Which was crazy because they did the same thing. Or maybe nearly the same: because the social technology was more responsive, less constrained. Blackberry failed because it assumed we would be grateful for the ability to send email and we would be loyal to the platform that provided it. But they were wrong: all we ever wanted was to communicate, and the platform or format was incidental. As communication was democratised through cheaper, more capable and rapidly expanding platforms and devices, suddenly that locked down, black plastic, out of date device languishing on the desk seemed ever more distanced from our everyday reality.

The devices and capability that organisations gave us was largely based on providing infrastructure, but it was wrapped up in a layer of control. There was always an underlying notion of ownership and servitude. But social technology removed and democratised that. And with that change, everything was up for grabs.

The office itself no longer offered exclusivity of infrastructure or opportunity. Instead, it came to be seen as outdated and insecure, buffeted by constant change projects and performance review that reduced us to one long battle for the next pay-rise. At the same time, the social connectivity enabled us to more easily build social reputation: suddenly it was much easier to learn, to share, to connect, to make sense of things, to get stuff done.

This is the reality of the Social Age: the four walls of the office and the paraphernalia it brought are redundant. We may still inhabit these spaces, but we don't have to. Wherever my iPad sits, that is where I can work is more important to me than a photocopier or car parking space.

And in the absence of security, the organisation needs to find new ways to engage the best talent and remain magnetic. It has to reflect the way that our career will be made up of multiple engagement, many jobs, changing over time. This change means that our loyalty must be earned, not assumed: it is bought through consistency of action over time, building trust, not by paying us or controlling us.

The conversations we have in the Social Age are fluid, moving between spaces easily. They are conversations that the organisation can listen to and be part of, but can no longer control.

The gadgets connect us into this community: they link us to people, knowledge, and capability. Technology measures things, shares things, captures and quantifies things. All at our fingertips, all democratised, all outside of organisational control.

So in a time where our career is our own, where nobody has ownership or responsibility for your long-term learning and development except yourself, it is these communities that are the only constant, coming with us from job to job, developing us throughout our lives.

In the Social Age, gadgets help us to learn and in the rest of this chapter, we will explore how.

THE FACILITATING NATURE OF TECHNOLOGY

In and of itself, it's nothing. Devices: just toys. Technology defined by dimensions, capabilities, megapixels and weight: the never ending quest for the lightest, highest definition, fastest and most pixelated format. But what it does is make us better: better able to do things, able to do new things, able to stop doing things that never added value.

Consider those dimensions a little more.

Technology lets us do things better: it enhances our capabilities. It lets us see further, hear more, reach out in different ways, connect across geographies and create effortlessly.

Technology lets us do new things, things we never thought possible. Like imaging the brain or travelling deep underwater. It lets us quest further and challenges our preconceptions.

Technology lets us stop doing things that never added value: this is a core feature of agility. An ability to be curious and challenge everything. I used to write by hand, not because I loved it, but because I had no option to type. Now I can type, it's both faster and clearer. So I don't really write anymore. Except Christmas cards. Writing was transient. What I really wanted to do was tell stories, and now I can do it faster and better.

The technology is often not the end in itself; it's the means by which we get there. Yet many organisations believe that the purchase is everything. They focus on the software or hardware, with the behaviours and desires as an afterthought.

But whilst technology facilitates us, it's rarely the whole story. We are superbly adapted to be adaptable! It's not a specific technology that is likely to be the answer, but rather what those technologies enable us to do. Take collaboration: many organisations choose a collaboration tool of choice, a particular system, and yet what's really important is the conversation, and that can happen through any channel. So instead of trying to own the system, they'd be better off helping us be better storytellers and let us figure the technology out ourselves.

It's a remnant of control behaviours. A belief that the technology is what's important and that we can fit people around it, whilst in fact it's just the thing that facilitates us to be better, to get things done.

So how do gadgets help us learn? By connecting us: by removing barriers to communication and allowing us to sidestep the rules.

NATIVE BEHAVIOURS

Gadgets help us to learn when they match up to our native behaviours: it's when we have to learn their rules that things go wrong. It's about the mindset of design: are we fitting into the native behaviours of people, or are we designing against features and expecting people to learn to fit against it?

Sure, sometimes we have to learn how to use new things, but often the learning is a sign of laziness in design. Or pointless innovation. Think back to our dimensions of technology: how much is something helping us do something better or stop doing something that's a waste of time? How much are we just introducing new noise into the system?

When we consider social technology, the clue is in the title: it's about social. It's about connections and conversations. It's not about features and sensors. The technology is important, but only as a means to an end. Social technology should facilitate conversations, through synchronous connectivity, ease of sharing, ability to add context and layers of interpretation and to show support and challenge. It shouldn't be about locking us into one channel or one technology. Let the conversation run free and feel the benefits.

COMMUNITY

The Social Age is lived within and alongside our communities. We engage in many different spaces for many different purposes, but with some commonality. Communities are the basic units of sense making: they help us figure out what to do and how to do it. But only if they are cohesive in values and purpose.

Consider those two things: shared value, shared purpose. Without them, there can be no coherence, no matter how good your technology. Gadgets can connect us to community, but they won't give it purpose and they won't make it cohesive. You can't build a technology for trust.

It works like this: there's a cost of membership. By being within a community, we align ourselves to shared purpose, common goals. But we may not be totally aligned: typically we are aligned enough to keep us engaged, but with areas of difference. Communities are thus cohesive, but with tolerance generated by these internal differences. Sub communities may form around these areas of difference (which can, in turn, lead to corrosive spaces if we are not careful, but that's a different story, not for here). If our views start to differ too widely from those of the community, we may either select ourselves out of it, or be selected out of it and given the boot. Coherence comes from the shared value: it's a direct foundation of the trust that's needed to fully engage in the space.

And purpose? Communities need purpose: it may be as prosaic as survival, or as specific as mapping the human genome. But the purpose contributes to unity and coherence.

So shared value and shared purpose: how are they reflected in technology? Often not at all is the answer: instead, we focus technology on membership, gamification and metrics, totally missing what gives a community is power and value. We worry about how people log in, how they retrieve their password or how we moderate their comments. But we don't worry about how they build trust and how we deal with the sub communities and their specific needs.

Gadgets connect us to our community: my phone links me to my Facebook community (and various 'pages', which house sub or parallel communities within it), as well as my Twitter community, the Wordpress one, LinkedIn, my Vine and SlideShare communities as well as less easily defined ones. Such as the community I would turn to for inspiration. Or for challenge. Or help.

We sometimes mistake the act of connection for the benefit derived, but in fact it's simply the conduit through which the conversations flow.

Communities drive change: they build consensus and share action. Technology supports this: consider the subversive role of communities and how it's enabled by gadgets.

Whilst today it's commonplace, the emergence of cameras on phones was neither assured nor widely welcomed. And yet it's transformed our storytelling ability and ability to influence community.

Capture, interpret, share.

The citizen journalist can capture easily, snapping away in a fully democratised manner, able to collect and curate linear sequences of imagery that document our days and tell visual stories that span the globe. The mechanisms of Social make images magnetic: we tag them and share them across platforms, with their associated short-form wisdom. The interpretation. Take a photo, add a tagline, who will question it? On the plus side, we can share learning fast. This type of image-based community sharing lets us build and permeate tribal knowledge in short and efficient order. But it also supports misinformation: images appropriated and misinterpreted, either by design or accident.

The speed and pace of sharing within our communities sometimes outstrips the speed of the truth. In training contexts, this is significant: a good story can travel faster than the official one. Communities are built to share and share at speed. Historically, there has always been how things are done by the rules, and how they are done in real life. The divergence was largely hidden and largely ignored. Today though, communities can subvert formal governance in short order, allowing the tribal wisdom to become both very public and dominant. The mindset for the organisation must be to get into the conversation, but no longer to try and own it.

This is the reality of the Social Age: communities taking on very real power and authority as their ability to build consensus and share meaning subverts more formal channels and hierarchies.

STORYTELLING

It starts with the weather: it's a bit dreary here today, low cloud giving the early morning sun a hazy and cold demeanour. How is it where you are? We start with the weather, we start small. Short stories that establish commonality, that build community. We don't start with the contentious: we build up to that slowly, once we have built coherence in the community, enough coherence to weather a bit of a storm.

We use stories in learning: to contextualise knowledge, to provide detail around process and method, to illustrate application. We use stories to share success and provide cautionary tales of failure.

Technology facilitates storytelling in all pervasive ways: it provides spaces for the stories to be shared, it provides tools to let us craft and illustrate them, it lets us take creative approaches to the style and shape of those stories and it democratises access to different media. Today, it's easy to use film, audio, imagery or text to tell our stories. We can do all those things from our phones and iPads. Things that once were the preserve of media companies and magazines are now easily within our grasp. The landscape of storytelling has been transformed by collaborative, social technology.

In learning, we use stories at different levels.

There's personal narrative, the #WorkingOutLoud approach that sees us create a day-by-day narrative of change. This may be conversational, almost synchronous: your sequence of status updates that, taken together, form a narrative of your story through the day, the week, the year.

Personal narratives are great for charting individual change and technology supports them in so many ways: it lets us snap away and capture the illustrations for our story. It lets us share those photos and add a commentary, choosing an appropriate tone of voice and audience. It lets us quantify our story: I cycled this far, I have a personal best, I beat you whilst I did it.

Technology used in this way is both documentary (this is what happened), creative (wasn't there a great view along the way) and predictive or aspirational (these are my goals that I'm counting down towards or earning badges to get...).

160

Above personal narratives are the co-created narratives that we form within communities: the conversations and 'sense making' activities that help us to be more effective.

Co-created narratives, the stories of communities, are about legacy. What did each cohort learn and what story did they share. Technology here is about providing space, but alongside that space, we have to give permission: permission to share, permission to learn, permission to make mistakes. When it comes to co-created group narratives, technology is only half the story: the permission we have to explore is the other half.

Finally, organisations have their own narratives: stories of their aspiration, how they want to be perceived. Organisational stories are usually broadcast: through their advertising and social media. They are rarely co-created but rather shaped, hones and broadcast. These are of less concern to us, because they are not stories of learning, but rather stories of aspiration.

So the gadgets we carry help us form and share our personal stories of learning, our co-created group 'sense-making' stories, and our organisational broadcasts. The devices themselves are almost irrelevant in terms of make, model and operating system: it's the facilitation of our storytelling behaviours that counts.

REPUTATION

In the Social Age, our reputation is based on our actions within and alongside our communities. Technology has made everything we do transparent: messages are amplified, travelling ever further and faster than ever before.

Reputation is the way the community views you and it's largely based on the consistency of your actions over time. If you are the person who is always the first to be critical, then that's your reputation, which may be ok, but which may erode your social authority: who wants to be the butt of your criticism next time?

The key element here is the amplification: the technology connects us to people, lets us push, retweet and forward things. It's the facilitating technology behind the actions that lets us shout with a louder voice or be heard by the most relevant people.

But of course it doesn't work all the time or for every story: amplification is highly selective. You can put out a thousand Tweets that never get read, or you can post one good picture or comment that goes around the world whilst you're fast asleep. It's to do with reputation, relevance, and ease of engagement and ease of sharing.

Some platforms are inherently social: typically your mobile phone, your tablet, your social media spaces and instant messaging. Others are inherently formal or more static: laptops that take an age to fire up, corporate intranets that are governed by social media policies, dinosaur systems for performance management or learning management. Whilst the technology doesn't guarantee how social a space will be, how widely your message will be amplified, the ease with which we learn or the relevance of the content, it can certainly ruin most of those things if it's badly designed or slow to access.

MEASUREMENT

If we can measure it, we can quantify the change, and if we can quantify the change, we can feel ourselves make progress. Which is nice. And makes it feel less like wasted effort...

Technology sits at the heart of this: we can use it for diagnostics, to quantify actions, to measure response times, to simulate situations or sensory inputs, to ping, poke and prod people, to play games, to score points and collect badges, to pedal further and faster and to navigate between waypoints whilst we do so. If there's one thing technology is good at, it's measuring.

Sometimes we even manage to measure the right things.

The misapplication of quantification is one of the greatest weaknesses in our relationship with learning technology. We measure stuff because we can, because we always have, or because we think we should, not because we're actually going to do something meaningful with the result.

Look at Strava: the cycling App that lets you chart your sector times on a ride against the community. It's meaningful, visual, competitive, motivational and simple to use. It measures and does something meaningful with the measurement (by interpreting it into a competition). Then look at much mobile learning rolled out in organisations: it's clunky, branded, written by committee, impractical, too long and often aimed at getting you to pass a test at the end to tick a box to fulfill a need. Someone else's need. Which do you think is more popular?

Gadgets help us learn when they create this type of meaning, when they interpret measurement itself into something that's more relevant and actionable than simple data.

Yet again, the technology will do whatever we tell it to do: the trick is to design the right applications and interpret the results correctly.

Look at psychometrics: many of these are now available online. You do the test, you get the result. But the result is meaningless without good interpretation, but often the feedback is given by the manager, who may have had no training in how to interpret it and, often as not, views it as 'pass' or 'fail'. The technology sits within an ecosystem and we have to consider every aspect of that ecosystem to truly find value.

We are at the start of our journey with wearable technology: today, much of it seems alien. I've spent the last year wandering around wearing my Google Glass, much of it apologetically, trying to find the point of it all.

But in three or five year's time, we will be immersed in a web of wearable technology and will be starting to see meaningful applications for learning. The quantification will be interpreted to be meaningful: to trigger the release of information or connect us to our communities in meaningful ways. It won't just measure where we've been and how hot it was, or the speed of the bike that got us there. It will add layers of information: you are in this building, so is John, who also has an interest in psychometric tools. Why don't you go talk to John: here's his location. Or maybe you're by a valve in an oil refinery and it pulls down relevant schematics, service history, photographs of common corrosion problems to look out for and some ideas for easy maintenance. And projects them all to your glasses.

Quantification is not the end game: it's another tool to deploy in service of helping people to be more effective. Not training them. Not testing them. Supporting them.

CONCLUSION

We've explored the ecosystem of the Social Age and the facilitating nature of technology: I've not talked about particular pieces of kit or particular brands, but rather a deconstruction of the more fundamental ways that gadgets help us to learn.

The conclusion? That gadgets facilitate learning, but that great learning design, storytelling, communication, sharing, collaboration and reflection are what gets the job done.

Technology is a means to an end, rarely an end in itself. We are too locked into the complexities and costs of buying new systems and technologies, which leads to the natural belief that they will solve our problems and last forever, both of which are fictions. In fact, we need a more lightweight approach: agile technologies to solve problems, interconnect, update and change and be disposed of at the end. Not one gadget to solve all our problems, but rather an ecosystem of interconnected technology and systems, each does their part, each easy to change.

The success of educational technology comes not from its features and functions. It comes from our ability to do something with it, to make a difference. To be agile.

CITATION

Stodd, J. (2015). How gadgets help us learn. In: Hopkins, D., ed., *The Really Useful #EdTechBook*, 1st ed. David Hopkins, pp.151-165.

STUDENTS LEADING THE WAY IN MOBILE LEARNING INNOVATION

TERESE BIRD

Educational Designer, School of Medicine, University of Leicester

@tbirdcymru

http://tbirdseyeview.wordpress.com/

Terese is currently working on curriculum design and mobile learning within the first UK Medical School to use iPads for learning at the undergraduate level. Recent funded research projects include EU-funded eMundus open educational practice project and evaluation of University of Leicester FutureLearn MOOCs, social media use by teachers and pupils, open education, open educational resources, e-books and e-readers, iTunesU in learning, webinars and multimedia. Particular interest in supporting researchers to digitally network and share their research, and in using VLE/LMS plus personal learning networks and social media to bridge the gap between students, and between student and tutor in distance learning contexts.

This chapter considers students' use of mobile devices - mobile phones and tablets - for their own learning. It comes out of research projects I've worked on within the UK higher education scene, beginning with evaluating podcasts and iPods in 2006 at Bangor University, through to the first e-readers in the UK in 2009, and up to the present one-iPad-per-student courses at University of Leicester as part of the Institute of Learning Innovation (originally Beyond Distance Research Alliance). I consider the question "*how do students come to use mobile devices to help their learning, and not just for their leisure?*" Do students need guidance to help them use these devices for learning? In many of the mobile learning cases I've worked on, students were given both the devices and guidance as to how the devices were intended to be used in their learning. These kinds of programmes are still rare amongst UK Higher Education (HE) courses. And yet they are relevant to, and throw light on, the whole issue of students' use of their own mobile devices, which we can expect will only increase as student ownership of good devices increases. This chapter will look at the ways HE students use mobile devices, both their own and supplied by the university, by examining four specific cases of mobile device use.

STUDENTS OWNERSHIP OF MOBILE DEVICES

Every recent survey of student ownership of mobile devices in the UK shows that a strong majority own smartphones, and growing numbers owning tablets. This alone should make university policy-makers consider whether and how they can leverage the power of these devices for the students' own learning, without need to purchase or do much training. Yet, when they intentionally decide to 'do mobile learning,' many university programmes and courses, including some at my university, choose to purchase a device for students. Why is this? It is usually for the ease of students using a single platform and single hardware, so that course material and course design can be planned and delivered for one platform. It is an amusing irony that Macintosh users, myself included, might have complained that their chosen operating system was ignored by university IT departments in the past, only to launch iPad-only courses in the mobile learning age, with similar arguments to the IT departments' insistence on supporting one platform. But I digress. As time goes on, most apps are being developed both for iOS and for Android, and other resources are web-based in HTML5, and hence platform and specific device choice should lessen as an issue.

The cases I discuss here include some in which students used only their own mobile devices, and some in which students were supplied with mobile devices. Even in the cases in which students were furnished with devices and given some specific guidance, they made the devices their own and came up with their own personalised ways of using them for their own study. For many, using these devices enabled independent study in new, engaging ways. Therefore, I can rightly title this chapter "*Students Leading the Way in Mobile Learning Innovation*". From these cases, I hope to draw commonalities and emerging principles which may help others considering whether and how to encourage students to use mobile devices in learning in their own contexts.

CASE 1: LECTURE PODCASTS AND MP3 PLAYERS

In 2006 in Bangor (Wales) University School of Psychology, Dr Jesse Martin and I collaborated to introduce both audio and video-enhanced podcasts of lectures. With the help of SionWyn Morris, David Robinson, and others, we installed our own 'home-built' lecture recording systems, a system we built ourselves rather than one of the commercial systems available now, in our lecture theatres. The resulting files were made available via the VLE (Virtual Learning Environment) Blackboard, in tandem with iTunes. Podcasts would just play if one clicked on the file in Blackboard, or would download if that was chosen, and a third choice was given which opened the podcasts as a series to be subscribed to, if the student had iTunes on her computer. Students also owned iPods and other brands of MP3 players, and were able to load the podcasts onto these. In 2006, iPod and MP3 players were not network-enabled; such devices needed to be physically connected to computers in order to receive audio files onto them. We gave no specific training for any of this. We posted on the VLE simple instructions to access the files on computers via the VLE, but no instructions for mobile device users. For those devices, the students figured everything out themselves. I recall that someone cautioned me against rolling out a programme without preparing explicit instructions in advance, because the students would get confused. But they did not get confused; I received no complaints or requests for training. This is not at all to belittle the wisdom of preparing and sharing good instructions for new learning innovations. I just didn't do it, and on this occasion, there were no ill effects. As for the lecture podcast project as a whole, it was very well received by the students, with some of them claiming whole-letter-grade improvements because of it. I relate findings from an online survey of students with particular questions designed to reveal how students use podcasts (.MP3 audio recordings) and vodcasts (video-enhanced podcasts, or videos comprised of the PowerPoint slides married together with lecturer's voice, saved as a .MOV or .MP4 file). The survey was completed in February 2008. Note that many of these findings are specifically about the use of the podcasts rather than the mobile devices. Regardless, conclusions can be drawn about the use of such devices in learning.

- 100% of self-identified respondents with disabilities reported that podcasts and vodcasts made a positive impact on both their learning experience and on their marks.
- Of those who did not identify themselves as having a disability, 90% said learning experience improved by using these files; 77% said marks improved with podcasts. With vodcasts, 95% of this same group said learning experience improved, and 90% said marks improved.
- When asked how they listen to/view podcasts and vodcasts,
    - Up to 80% said they viewed online in the browser
    - Up to 30% said they viewed or listened on MP3 player
    - 90% said they downloaded the files to their own computer. This supported my hypothesis that podcasts and vodcasts have a particularly useful affordance in that they are portable and downloadable, and can be listened to and viewed away from the Internet.
- 15% of podcast-users and 22% of vodcast-users claimed they regularly used the files to catch up on missed lectures. While there was no question in the survey which may indicated whether or not missing lectures would be a deliberate choice given the existence of the files, the numbers suggest that there is at least the possibility students may make that choice.
- 92% of vodcast-users and 90% of podcast-users claimed that they listened to/viewed the lecture multiple times.
- 58% of podcast-users and 67% of vodcast-users claimed that they regularly listened to/viewed the lecture files with full attention. And 61% of podcast-users and 56%of vodcast-users claimed to regularly write additional notes while doing this. It is very interesting to consider that in this case, writing notes had a completely different purpose than has writing notes in a live lecture. In a live lecture, one main purpose of writing is to record what the lecturer says. Whilst listening to a podcast of a recorded lecture, a student is synthesizing and processing knowledge. This suggests that podcasts and vodcasts support lectures by giving students a new vehicle by which they may process the knowledge gained

from lectures. (Bird, T., Morris, S.W., Martin, J., Browbridge, J., Gill, T., 2008).

These data were gathered as part of a project funded by the Higher Education Academy Psychology Subject Centre (1).

CASE 2: SONY E-READERS FOR MASTERS DISTANCE LEARNERS

In 2009, as part of the University of Leicester Beyond Distance Research Alliance, I began working on the DUCKLING project (2), a JISC-funded 'Transforming curriculum delivery' project. Amongst other interventions, we transformed instructor-written learning material into EPUB eBooks, loaded them onto university-purchased Sony e-readers (the Kindle was not yet available in the UK), and shipped them to distance students located around the world. This was done for two Masters-level distance programmes, one in Occupational Psychology and one in Education for the Teaching of English as a Second Language. We prepared simple instructions on how to use the e-reader and how to find the different readings. We printed these instructions and included them in the shipment to the students, and also posted them onto Blackboard in a special discussion group for discussing the e-readers. As time went on, we noticed that students were asking on Blackboard how to add additional readings onto their e-readers. I posted some instructions. I then noticed that other student's added additional suggestions, such as good sites for free academic material in eBook formats, and how to put the readings onto other devices such as iPhones and Kindles. We could see that students were developing their own ways of studying, making use of the e-readers' affordances. In my mind, this was a proof-of-concept that e-readers could be well utilised in higher education for academic reading, and could specifically serve busy and motivated postgraduate students who often work full-time and must squeeze in bits of study time when they can. In terms of supporting the students, we gave them simple initial guidance, and they just ran with it. Table 1 gives the main benefits students experienced from using e-readers in their course. The main negative students found with the e-readers were that they could not take notes directly onto the files.

Functionalities/features of e-book reader that support effective reading	Findings	Key points
Portability Small, compact size Lightweight	Increasing mobility and flexibility	Students used their e-book readers in different places: at home, in the office, in public places (e.g. in Cafés and parks), and on the move (e.g. on aeroplanes and trains).
Readability under different conditions	Saving costs and resources	Students become less dependent on printed material and more selective in printing material out, resulting in saving costs and resources.
Accessing all course material from one device Accessing course material without the internet connection	Making better use of time	It's easier to take the e-book reader anywhere and read whenever students have a minute. It enables students to fill in the gaps during the day.
Continue reading and Bookmark functions Long battery life Capacity to accommodate many readings User-friendly interface	Optimising study strategy	Some students changed strategies for reading and approaches to assignments as a result of having an e-book reader.

Table 1. Summary of benefits of e-book readers to student learning.

(Nie, 2010, p.11)

CASE 3: IPADS FOR DISTANCE CRIMINOLOGY MASTERS STUDENTS IN WAR ZONES

In March 2012, the University of Leicester's Department of Criminology launched a new distance-learning course, the Masters in Security, Conflict, and International Development. Students enrolling on this course were likely to be professionals living and working in areas of the world, which had recently experienced conflict, and were therefore not likely to be able to access the Internet more often than once or twice a month. The department, however, wished to offer students richer learning materials than just printed text. They decided to commission an App and send each student an iPad. The App consists of audio, video, and text, which do not normally require persistent Wi-Fi to run. The App, entitled SCID, is available for free in the Apple App store, but only a fraction of the learning material is accessible before a university username and password are required, which are only given upon payment of tuition fees. Students receive their iPad from the university along with simple instructions, download the App, and are able to study from their iPad regardless of the lack of Internet connectivity. Students are also sent Amazon gift vouchers and instructed to download the Kindle App and use the vouchers for books on the reading list. This system and the programme has been deemed so successful that the department is beginning to extend the App + iPad model to the rest of their distance learning programmes. This initiative was evaluated and reported by Institute of Learning Innovation as part of a JISC-funded Transformation Project, Places *(3)*.

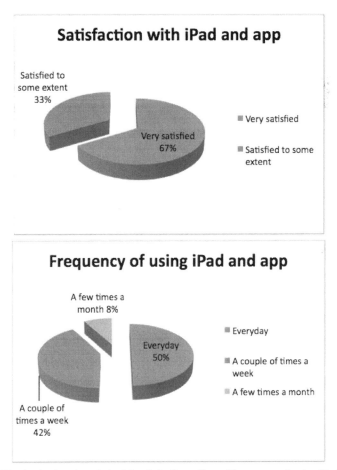

Figure 1. Pie charts showing students' satisfaction with and frequency of using iPad and App for studies in the Criminology Security, Conflict, and International Development course (Nie et al, 2012, pp. 5, 6)

Table 2 (below) illustrates the different benefits to study which the students commented on, each with an example quote taken from a student survey. (Nie et al, 2012)

IPAD & APP BENEFITS TO STUDY	ILLUSTRATIVE QUOTE FROM STUDENT
Study on the move	*"For me, the course App is suitable based on the nature of my job which demands me to always be on the move. Print could be very bulky for me to move."*
Study offline	*"Often my Internet is of a poor standard so the App makes it easier to study without having to wait for the page to load."*
Time management	*"Having access to the information wherever I go has allowed for better time management particularly as a distance learning student and under full time employment."*
Motivation and engagement	*"Firstly I am more motivated, as it is structured and organised. I am getting through more than I would if I was solely given a recommended reading list."*
Skills development	*"I have found the course material, the iPad and [the] Blackboard all very useful. It is forcing me to maintain pace with technology, a point I needed to with having two boys both studying at the 6th form and university respectively. I am really enjoying using and blending all the teaching methods available."*

Table 2. iPad and App study benefits and student quotes, from the Criminology Security, Conflict, and International Development course

In addition to the course app, students reported using other apps for their study, including: PDF Readers, Kindle App, Twitter (following a course Twitter account), Pages, Evernote, iTunesU, Skype (communication with tutor and other students), iBrainstorm, Dropbox, and Blackboard Mobile Learn. Learning to use these Apps in their learning was also seen by the students as contributing to their skills development.

CASE 4; IPADS FOR MEDICAL UNDERGRADUATE STUDENTS

In autumn 2013, the University of Leicester School of Medicine decided to give one iPad to each undergraduate first year student. As of this writing, this Medical school is the only one in the UK giving iPads to its undergraduate students. The driver for this decision was the need to quickly update workbooks which had been previously printed for the students. Given the speed at which information requires updating (very often), and the expense and hassle of printing (too much), together with the need for students to have learning material at hand anytime anywhere, it seemed that giving students iPads on which they could read and take notes on the material was a sensible, while admittedly expensive, option.

Students were given simple guidance to download an App (Notability) to read and take notes on their workbooks which were furnished in PDF format, and establish a Dropbox account, as well as to bring their iPad to every learning session. The workbooks, some as long as 100 pages or more, were distributed to the students via the VLE (Blackboard); no paper workbooks were issued. Lecture presentations were also distributed to students in PDF format, usually before the lecture. Students participated in online surveys (via Blackboard) at the beginning, middle, and end of the year, and were also invited to email short descriptions of how they were using their iPad for study, several times during a specific week in May 2014. From these data captures, a picture could be formed of how the students were using their iPads to study.

Survey 1 with 11 questions was completed in October 2013 by 103 students. Survey 2 with 12 questions was completed on 25 December 2013 and N=88 students completed. There are a total of 233 first year students; all were invited to participate in these surveys. The surveys asked different questions, with some overlap. Figure 2 pictures the replies to a Survey 1 question about overall satisfaction with iPad for learning.

"Overall, I am satisfied with using the iPad to enhance my learning in this course."

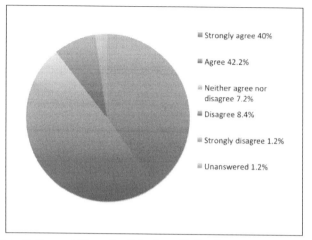

Figure 2. Survey 1 "Overall satisfaction with iPad" question and replies

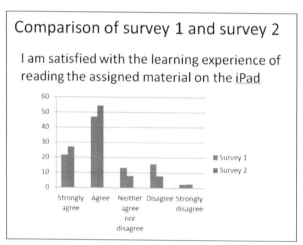

Figure 3. Comparison of replies to the statement "I am satisfied with the learning experience of reading the assigned material on the iPad" occurring in surveys 1 and 2.

Figure 3 compares the results in the two surveys, to the question of whether the iPad served well for reading. A modest increase in both "strongly agree" and "agree" can be seen between Survey 1 (October) and Survey 2 (December), while a corresponding modest decrease can be seen in both "disagree' and "strongly disagree." These data suggest overall satisfaction with the iPad as a learning tool -- satisfaction which grew as time passed. But in what ways were the iPads being used for learning, beyond simply being used as an e-reader? The free-comment questions of the surveys help answer this question.

In Survey 1, the question *"Please tell us any further comments about the experience of reading and annotating on the iPad"* yielded some insights into iPad affordances and how students were using them to learn. 73 out of total 233 students commented. Table 1 shows how many occurrences of each keyword or topic were mentioned, with a note of the pedagogical and practical purpose of the activity, along with arising issues noted by students.

NUMBER OF COMMENTS	TOPIC OF KEYWORD	WHAT STUDENTS ARE DOING TO LEARN WITH IPAD OR ISSUES ARISING, RELATED TO TOPIC OR KEYWORD
31	Lectures	• Download lecture PDF onto iPad to read before lecture • Arrange and organise in Dropbox • Take notes onto lecture PDF (some commented they could not keep up typing) • Review lecture notes whilst listening to MP3 of lecture
18	Workbooks	• Add notes and answer questions into PDF workbooks using Notability, other PDF App • Arrange and organise in Dropbox • Add new self-discovered material into provided workbook
17	Group work	• Organise and storing group work answers (see Figure 3) • Search Internet for info during sessions • Some comments that paper is easier to record what the group discusses and learns
15	Preference for paper or handwriting	• Comments that at least in some cases, paper or handwriting is preferred
12	Switching between Apps	• Difficulty switching between Apps or documents

6	eBooks	• Mostly positive comments about convenience of having eBooks from reading list in one device, in searchable format
4	Stylus	• Positive comments using stylus to write and draw
2	Math Calculation	• Negative comments – iPad not good at this
2	Keyboard	• Helpfulness of external keyboards

Table 3. Further comments about the experience of reading and annotating on the iPad, from Survey 1, organised by keyword or topic, with descriptive details.

Figure 4. Workbooks, lecture files, and other learning material organised and colour-coded on student iPads, in a groupwork session.

The email survey conducted during one week in May 2014 yielded richer data and insight into how the students used the iPads. The students were asked to email us as often as they wished during the week: "*a brief update on how you are using your iPad at that moment (a bit like a Facebook status update). We would be really interested to find out the following:*

- *Where you are using the iPad (home, café, pub, train etc)?*
- *Are you just working by yourself or with friends?*
- *What apps are you using and how these have helped you achieve what you wanted to do?*
- *Anytime you are sharing info or connecting with other students (and how you are doing this)?*
- *Screen shots of apps/anything useful?*
- *Photos that tell us what you are doing (no identifiable people)?*
- *Anything else you think might be helpful?"*

We received 136 emails during the week. Most were short descriptions of what they were doing, where, with whom. Some were long descriptions of their studies using iPads throughout the day. Images and snapshots were included in a few cases. The following are emerging themes and findings:

GROUP WORK

One feature of Medical students using iPads is group work. In the University of Leicester Medical School, first year undergraduates attend sessions in which they are divided into groups of about 8. As a group, they work on questions and problems. Often they create a Facebook group, and meet outside of class sessions to study as a group. 22% of responses to our Gmail survey referred to group work using their iPads. Examples of how they conducted group study, both in class and outside class, with their iPads, include:

- One person looks at the workbook (on Notability) on iPad, asks a question to the group, and passes on the iPad to another group member for another quiz question.
- Using Google Drive to collaborate remotely with another student
- Sharing notes and images with others in study group, via email, Facebook, iMessage
- Sharing group work answers between groups, using Airdrop
- Everyone in group has their iPad, studying and discussing together, outside class
- One person creates flash cards on Brainscape or Anki App to test group

members

- Students discuss the topic and develop the case as a spider diagram, which is photographed with group members' iPads and then added to later, individually (see Figure 5).

Figure 5. Students in a group work session develop a case as a spider diagram, which is then photographed on individuals' iPads for their own further development later.

LOCATION

In the Gmail survey, we asked students to state where they were studying with their iPads. Students mention that they study in their home, in their kitchen, at friend's home, in a campus building, in the university or public library, on the bus, on the train, in a coffee shop, outdoors, at the university botanical garden. One student described studying in a specific computer laboratory, where the computers were so slow that s/he pushed aside the keyboard, and pulled out iPad, pen, and pad of paper to study with those tools instead. Whether or not there is good Wi-Fi is an issue closely related to location. Sometimes students mentioned that there was no or poor Wi-Fi where they would be studying, and they would have to work around this with their iPad by choosing apps which do not require persistent Wi-Fi. Sharing documents with each other via Airdrop is a common workaround for no Wi-Fi, for example, as is saving reading material into Adobe Reader in advance of a bus journey.

HANDWRITING AND DRAWING

In the first survey in autumn 2013, 15 students commented that at least in some situations, they would prefer to use paper to read from or write onto. In some of these comments, handwriting is the focus of their comment. Writing by hand was seen to be quicker than typing, and seen by some to aid their recall of what they wrote. In the Gmail survey, three students mentioned using Penultimate, an App that allows handwritten notes to be saved in Evernote and later searched. In more than one survey, students mentioned drawing as a way of processing what they had learnt perhaps in the dissection room (where iPads are prohibited) and from lectures. Figure 6 consists of one student's study drawings. Some students mentioned the brands of stylus they purchased, mostly on the inexpensive side.

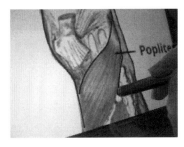 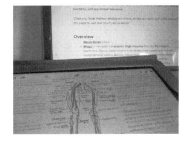

Figure 6. Medical student's drawings on iPad

APPS AND WEBSITES

The following apps and websites were mentioned in the email survey, in descending order by number of mentions:

1. Notability - PDF reader and annotating
2. Brainscape - make your own flashcards
3. Essential Anatomy 3D - anatomy images and quizzes
4. TeachMeAnatomy - online anatomy encyclopedia

5. Safari - iPad browser

6. YouTube - for visuals of conditions, anatomy, procedures

7. Pages - word processor for iPads and Macs

8. Anatomy Quiz - anatomy quizzes

9. iMessage - iPad message app

10. Dropbox - cloud storage

11. Penultimate - handwriting app, syncs to Evernote

12. Blackboard - mobile App for Blackboard VLE

13. OSCE Skills - tutorial App supporting Objective Structured Clinical Exams

14. Muscle and Bone Anatomy

15. Facebook - mentioned as facilitator for group discussion and also as a distraction

Other Apps which were each mentioned once: 3D4Medical (actually a company producing many anatomy Apps), Adobe Reader (eBook reader,) Airdrop, Anatomy, Anki (flashcards), Essential Skeleton, Google Drive, Gray's Anatomy, iBooks, Inkling (eBook platform), Instant Anatomy, iPhoto (to photograph slides in lecture), iTunes, Keynote, Medline For OSCE, Muscles Pro, NetAnatomy, Numbers (used to graph answers in group work), Radio App, Resuscitation, Screenshot, SimpleMind (Mindmap App), Visible Bodies, Word.

DISCUSSION

In all of these situations, the mobile devices, even if they were originally furnished by the institution, were in the end owned by the students. In all cases, the university furnished learning material in mobile-ready formats and encouraged the students to use this material. Therefore it was generally in the students' best interests to use their mobile devices with these materials.

In all of these cases, the question arises of student motivation. Why did the students use the mobile devices? With the possible exception of some students in Case 3, students were not compelled or required to use the mobile devices, although all were encouraged to do so. Some of the students were campus-based, others were distance only. Some were undergraduates, others were postgraduates. Some were traditional-age students, others were more mature. Regardless, in every case, students saw something in the use of the mobile devices which would enhance and improve their learning, and something they could personally develop for their own learning. I think I can see common aspects among the cases, and come to some principles for successful mobile learning.

Educators must make mobile learning:

- **Easy** - In all of the above cases, care was taken that access to the learning materials via the mobile devices was a simple matter. Testing was done in advance and simple instructions given, to smooth the way. Cautionary tales are often told of interactive whiteboards in UK schools in years past. These fell out of favour because they were just too tricky for busy educators to get to grips with. Mobile devices or Apps will only be welcomed if they are easy to use, by both students and staff.
- **Attractive** - In all of these cases, students commented about enjoying the use of the device, and/or about the attractiveness of the learning materials. One reason why Apple products have become so pervasive is due to the company's attention to design and goal of making use of their products a pleasant experience. Our learning materials and their presentation on mobile devices should do likewise.
- **Downloadable** - It is fascinating that struggling with Wi-Fi has been a mobile learning issue in the University of Leicester medical school as well as in conflict zones of the world. In all four cases, a key affordance of the learning materials was that they could be downloaded, so that students at least had the option of reading/listening/viewing on the device itself, away from the Internet and regardless of persistent Wi-Fi. This is where current popular VLEs are not quite mobile-ready yet; they seem to be dependent on a live Wi-Fi connection which is just not always feasible. Therefore mobile learning cannot be assumed to be handled fully by the VLE; educators need to consider our materials and make them downloadable at least some of the time.
- **Expected** - We educators can create the environment for students to be learning independently on their own devices, by encouraging it and pointing them in the right direction to get started, and giving them the

impression that it is not required but somewhat expected that they will be learning on their mobiles. Mobile devices and digital media are the mass communication of the 21st century; there is no question that students are using these devices now and will be in their future careers. It is only to their advantage that they feel au fait with using them for professional and academic purposes. If we as educators feel we need a bit of help with this task, this is where a friendly learning technologist comes in handy. Learning technologists understand both pedagogical and technological issues and are invaluable for planning, testing and implementing mobile learning and other educational technology interventions.

Students learn best when the method or device is chosen and/or personalised by them, when they have made it their own for their independent learning. Mobile learning can be a powerful tool for personalised and independent learning. I hope these cases offer ideas and principles to help enable mobile learning that is fruitful and enjoyable for both staff and students.

NOTES

1. Higher Education Academy Psychology Subject Centre: https://www.academia.edu/1099559/Using_enhanced_and_video_podcasts_of_lecture_recordings_to_support_student_learning_implementation_and_evaluation

2. DUCKLING Project: http://webarchive.nationalarchives.gov.uk/20140702233839/http://www.jisc.ac.uk/whatwedo/programmes/elearning/curriculumdelivery/duckling.aspx

3. PLACES project; http://www2.le.ac.uk/departments/beyond-distance-research-alliance/projects/places?uol_r=464f5944

REFERENCES

Bird, T., Morris, S. W., Martin, J., Brownbridge, J., Gill, T. (2008) Using enhanced and video podcasts of lecture recordings to support student learning: implementation and evaluation | Terese Bird - Academia.edu, [online] Available from: http://www.academia.edu/1099559/Using_enhanced_and_video_podcasts_of_lecture_recordings_to_support_student_learning_implementation_and_evaluation (Accessed 29 August 2013).

Nie, A. M., Bird, T., Beck, A., Hayes, N. and Conole, G. (2012) Adding Mobility to Distance Learning PLACES Case Study Background Aims and Objectives JISC Resources / Technology Used, [online] Available from: http://www2.le.ac.uk/departments/beyond-distance-research-alliance/projects/places .

Nie, M. (2010) A case study of integrating e-book readers into two Masters' distance learning programmes in Occupational Psychology, Leicester, UK, [online] Available from: http://www2.le.ac.uk/departments/beyond-distance-research-alliance/projects/duckling/E-book reader for OP.pdf .

CITATION

Bird, T. (2015). Students leading the way in mobile learning innovation. In: Hopkins, D., ed., *The Really Useful #EdTechBook*, 1st ed. David Hopkins, pp.167-185.

TECH DANDY, AND THE ART OF LEISURE LEARNING

INGE DE WAARD

Researcher (Athabasca University, Canada; The Open University, UK; and Institute Tropical Medicine, Belgium)

@Ignatia

http://ignatiawebs.blogspot.co.uk/

As a doctorandus I am affiliated with The Open University of the United Kingdom, working on heutagogy and self-determined learning of online learners. In the past I have been the eLearning coordinator at the Institute of Tropical Medicine in Belgium for which I started and coordinated multiple mobile and online projects. In 2013 I finished mobile/MOOC research at Athabasca University, Canada looking at the impact of mobile access on MOOC learner interactions. I am a reviewer for multiple online learning journals, a member of different online learning organizations and I share new insights or experiences through my blog.

In this technology driven world people are often referred to as geeks, nerds, academics, or any type of description pointing towards a dry, rather rational personality. Now it is time to reveal one of EdTech human resource secrets: the Tech Dandy. We - the in-crowd of the worldwide training web - can spot a Tech Dandy from afar. It is only logical, for we are Tech Dandy pioneers. Now it is time to share the Art of Leisure Learning with the world.

This chapter puts the Tech Dandy in the spotlight, and shares how to inspire other learners to become experienced Tech Dandies and learn at the speed of light while always looking cool, collected and calm. The Tech Dandy has a natural charm to him or her, and uses tech in a suave, organic way to satisfy an ever present learning desire. Leisure learning is a way of life, it is an Art. But becoming a charismatic leisure learner, a real Tech Dandy, demands intelligence, planning, digital skills, gallant communication, and most of all an in-depth understanding of Apps,

Once you are a full-fledged Tech Dandy, it will be easy to put your own Leisure Learning practice into any training or online course design and optimize the world for your learners.

TO CURATE IS TO LIVE LEISURELY

Tech Dandies understand the importance of living in the middle of a personal network, they use Apps for their own merriment, and their knowledge is fed with a constant stream of handpicked, as well as serendipitous information of the highest quality.

A DANDY LIVES AMONG THE BEST

Establishing or maintaining yourself as a Tech Dandy demands a carefully planned effort. First of all you need to build an information web with you at the center. This information stream of high quality news will be the core of your ongoing development, and helps you set up a long-term, well-connected learning network.

First of all roam social media (if you do not know what social media is, close this chapter and please return to your simple life and come back once you hear your true Tech Dandy calling). You can start weaving your network by using selected hashtags in your field of interest (e.g. #lrnchat, #mlearning or #quantifiedself). If someone is talking or writing interestingly on that subject, 'follow' them. Once you feel confident, start a conversation with those experts so you can learn from them and become wiser yourself. Your network will grow, your knowledge will strengthen.

NETWORKS CATAPULT YOU TO YOUR GOALS

We are all Learning for our own leisure and profession, as such it is important to use the intelligence of others to direct us towards what we need to know, but were not (yet) aware of. One of today's options is to engage in a community that works in a similar field, and wants to share resources and learning pathways, and to implement the right tools to enable this type of informal knowledge and learning exchange. *(1)*.

CURATION IS CAPITAL

Once your network is started, and your information stream is fed with relevant online sources, you will have a good starting point for curating your own knowledge channel. Curation demands that you select the best and most inspiring articles, media, and ideas from your news stream and you add a bit of yourself to it. For example: you collect all there is to know about the Flipped classroom approach *(2)*, and you add either your own ideas, or much better: your own experience to those articles while posting them to the broader public.

Second, start to read journals, news sites, wikis, blogs, online magazines… and add anything that makes you tick to your own media channel or content curation tool (e.g. Hootsuite, Pinterest, Storify, Scoop.it).

TUNE INTO TECH-POP MAGAZINES, BUT ADD A BIT OF SPICE

As a Tech Dandy you need to build your post-post renaissance wo/man knowledge. To do so successfully, a nice curation of trendy online, tech magazines can help you stay on top of what is happening in the tech world. Some options are: Wired *(3)*, Mashable *(4)*, The/Intercept *(5)*, and of course Huffington post/education *(6)* for overall and tech interests. And all of them spiced up with educational goodies that can be found on: Educause *(7)*, the Learning Solutions magazine *(8)*, and of course the inspiring Ol'Daily *(9)*.

No curated stream is worth anything without a good deal of Twitter news. You can easily enhance your daily information blessings with: @BrainPickings, @TheScienceGuy, @museumnerd, @mental_floss and of course your own curated Twitter list of 'keypeople'.

189

Last but not least there is one superb gathering of all the hottest educational news and that is … well no, sorry about that. A Tech Dandy does not reveal all of his/her sources, that would take the fun out of serendipitous exploring.

DO NOT TAKE 'YOUR LOCATION' BY DEFAULT

As a Tech Dandy you travel the world, maybe not always in the flesh, but at least virtually. One easy to adjust tech fact is 'location'. It gives a bit of a global feel to your Twitter, Instagram, Google search stream. For example, I often change my Twitter location to another city, e.g. Honolulu, Hawaii (well, Honolulu, US as Twitter location is sometimes tricky). This allows me to see what is tweeting there, and it offers a nice way to connect to my network of peers living in that area.

THE MOBILE LIFESTYLE

As digital nomads we wander about the virtual and global world, trying to find meaning and a balanced way of (professional) living. Being mobile is both living a mobile life (either roaming the globe in search for meaningful conferences, seminars, or EdTech pop-up events; either in person or virtual), and being equipped with mobile devices. This combination makes us in to those technology enhanced learning professionals whose expertise is distributed over time and space.

If technology is like a seventh sense, the ultimate mobile instrument is always within your grasp, or at least it is there when you wish it to be. Leisure learning becomes so much easier with a mobile device in your pocket. You can follow educational discussions (e.g. #lrnchat), share experiences *(10)*, and enroll in online courses to learn-as-you-go (e.g. MOOC). Sharing will result in more connections, more conversations, and a stronger network.

Content production is benevolent for all. As such a Tech Dandy takes pictures, narrates experiences and adventures via blogs, Instagram, and any type of current preferred mobile and connected tool. Leaving nuggets of wisdom as true breadcrumbs for others to offer them shared learning paths and insights.

MOOC-ALICIOUS

MOOCs are all around us. Massive Open Online Courses (MOOC) are mostly free and you can choose from a wide variety of platforms (Coursera, Iversity, FutureLearn, EdX, Udacity, Canvas.net...). MOOC learning is true leisure learning. You can screen the courses that are coming up and you can register for those that you think will be either useful professionally or inspiring personally. Once the course starts, you screen the topics of each week and you make a decision: either follow the full course (with or without some sort of certification), or select only those weeks during which a specific subject matter is presented. This modus operandi saves you time and increases the leisure time in your learning journey. At the same time you can leisurely pick up bits and pieces that will make you in to the all-round, renaissance Tech Dandy you want to be.

MOOCs are everywhere, and as such Tech Dandies are often pioneering new learning technologies, including setting up alternative MOOCs, building mash-ups on the outskirts of the web to attract other Tech's of every identity, and of course trying out the latest start-up goodie bags released as closed beta releases. Socrates knew it, we know it, only by actually walking the walk and to boldly go where no wo/man has gone before can we truly feel the benefits, challenges or downsides of any educational technology. As such each Tech Dandy is a conscious part of the whole crowd, an active part of the intelligent swarm. We are connected, our voices are heard, and our network appreciates our ideas and trustworthiness. Charm can only survive in a warm, yet honorable learning ecology build upon trust and openness.

COMFORTABLE OFF- AND ONLINE

No matter how much information floats around us, a Tech Dandy is never stressed. The Tech Dandies leisure learning environment is so well organized, that we can choose between being on- or offline. There is no pressure, thanks to an intelligently crafted information stream, combined with an open mindset, believing in serendipitous knowledge creation by dipping in and out of the constant stream of information that surrounds each one of us.

Serendipitous learning is a nice companion for any tech professional. While roaming the web, answers are found to new and old questions, each time in a variety of stories. By constantly selecting those answers with the highest quality the Tech Dandy practices her or his critical thinking, sharpening the ever evolving mind. But in order to enable our brain to process all these ideas, suggestions, learning models, and frameworks it is pivotal that disconnected time is planned. Finding a nice balance in life and work is essential to radiate calm, and as such it is just as important to switch between mental and physical work to keep a mind in a sound body (Iuvenalis: mens sana, in corpore sano) as it is to switch between on- and off-life.

A NOSE FOR NEUROSCIENCE

With the human brain being increasingly dissected and understood, neuroscience has become one of the tools of the training trade. In fact with the concepts of neuroscience at their best, it is a pleasure to see how education can be reshaped in a creative and cognitively stimulating way *(11 and 12)*. Education and training no longer exist as a separate identity - it never was - but with the increased speed of research and technology, one cannot ignore the upcoming scientific fields that are increasingly inspiring technology enhanced learning, such as neuroscience.

ONLINE EDUCATION IS IN CONTINUAL BETA

With online education as a main expertise, it is important to acknowledge the continual beta of EdTech. Online education is constantly evolving, and the technological universe is expanding at such an enormous rate that it can take out the best of us, but … as a Tech Dandy you simply gather a few of top notch, easy to use websites that are curated by others to keep on top of your field.

- A wiki focusing on learning theories *(13)*
- A good page to emerge and find topics or details on instructional design

(14)

- Wiki devoted to Blooms digital taxonomy *(15)*
- Or simply some good old research journals, all open access of course: IRRODL *(16)*

And of course a bit of http://scholar.google.com will do nicely as well. Don't forget that truly understanding a tool saves time and adds radiance to any EdTech professional. To get that bit of extra, I regularly tweak the advanced settings of Google Scholar to find papers in different languages, thus expanding my horizon, and keeping my non-native languages in a fresh, professional condition. It also helps to find local research for those moments where you are asked to provide advice for an international firm or organization. Local, contextualized projects are always more inspiring and will instill more trust in you and your work. Savoir vivre also compliments professional life.

Professional jargon is quintessential to any Tech Dandy.

GESTURE BASED LEARNING, META GLASSES ... DAILY VOCABULARY

Although there is a lot you can do or leave as a Tech Dandy, you cannot ignore upcoming trends and even the most geeky of educational hypes. An easy way to keep on top of what is and where it might go, is a smart (and not too time intensive) idea to read the New Media Consortium publications, featuring the Horizon Report *(17)*. This report is published around the first quarter of the year, and it provides an easy access, example filled overview of the hottest and upcoming educational technologies.

Nice, and easy-peasy-lemon-squeezy.

Just for fun let's look at two nice and serious EdTech options that are on the rise.

- *Gesture based learning* is getting more and more attention. Gesture-based learning uses interfaces where the human body interacts with digital resources without using the common devices such as a keyboard or mouse. Kinect from xBox brought this invention to a broader market. It is an upgrade to the virtual systems dating back from the nineties, and which are now enabling to move and select virtual objects or content in a 3D setting. A trick already featured in multiple Sci-Fi movies, e.g. The Day the Earth Stood Still (1951 original version: yes, that early), Johnny Mnemonic (1995), Minority Report (2002), Iron Man (2008), Star Trek (2009).

- *Meta glasses (18)* are of course the new high end virtual glasses, positioning themselves as superior Google glasses, and enabling augmented learning, production and design. Pricy though, but as a Tech Dandy, you do not talk about money, only frontier EdTech solutions. Having said that, for approximately 25 USD/EUR you can buy a cardboard virtual set up for your mobile and … explore the virtual world for its educational values. *(19)*

DARING DATA

Big data might cover any subject, for educational purposes it is better to talk about evidence based learning analytics. In this day and age a lot of our movements and actions can be quantified and that is certainly the case for each of our own learning. As such the field of evidence based learning analytics paved the way for a better understanding of each of our own learning path (breadcrumbs we leave on social media, in MOOC platforms, on discussion forums…). Nevertheless, our personal, informal learning is still mostly done outside of the 'formal' learning analytics vision (despite wonderful efforts of xAPI - *20)* and learning locker *(21)*. And as real Tech Dandies do, we simply peruse the MOOC platforms to find new big data and data analytic courses, and we hook up through our personal learning network to other, more experienced learning analytic gurus.

Learning analytics are being taken up by Higher Ed as a priority, as access and control of learning data will give insights to a more broader spectrum of learning, teaching, and training. Data are not only limited to the rational data that immediately comes to mind, but also to emotional data that influences all of our motivational and practical drives towards conquering knowledge and wisdom. A nice starting point to gain insights in learning analytics is the Learning Analytics and

Knowledge (LAK) conference, with free conference proceedings to dive into *(22)*, or have a look at the Learning Analytics Community Exchange report on measuring and understanding learner emotions (by Bart Rienties and Bethany Alden Rivers, and online - *23*).

WEARABLE YOU

As a Tech Dandy it might be a far stretch to keep a cool pose after a serious physical workout. Instagram might not be the way to go when you are all sweaty; nevertheless wearables are part of every EdTech persona, including us Tech Dandies. If you want to explore the realms of game based learning, the easiest way to boldly go where others have just started to go before is to jump off the deep end, into your own quantified self. The quantified self is the full set of digital data that you can radiate while being on- or offline, in most cases the offline parts involve wearable technology. With these wearables you can adjust your sleeping pattern (thus ensuring a fabulous presence at all times), you can engage in friendly jogging competitions with people that live or work in the same area by comparing each other's jogging patterns and results, or you can simply use it to optimize work patterns.

There are of course a lot of wearable options out there, and the easy to wear options vary from fitness bands to smartwatches. To me the best casual chic can be found in the smartwatch. You simply wear it on your wrist like any other watch, and it tells you when you are tagged in social media tools, or when you get messages, mails, and other communications, and even results on a range of live data streams.

If you are ever asked to instill some extra energy in a corporation, simply introducing wearables as ways to get some friendly competition going on the work floor, will give rise to some healthy office competition. For example: how much exercise during your office hours results in improved mental work? This casual introduction to evidence based analytics and friendly competition will ensure a healthy lifestyle for all. Is not that just dandy?

IN CONCLUSION

The Art of Leisure Learning is all about obtaining pure knowledge, to disseminate that real knowledge and transmit it to your peers, or embed it in your future learning solutions will ensure high quality returns.

For a Tech Dandy an air of expertise is simply not enough. A Tech Dandy is an expert, but with an aura of cool accompanying evidence-based training knowledge. Knowledge creation is taking educational Art to the point of perfection, and leisure learning is the action accompanying the Art.

NOTES

1. Pathfinder: http://www.pathgather.com/

2. Flipped Learning: http://flippedlearning.org/

3. Wired: http://www.wired.com/

4. Mashable: http://mashable.com/

5. The/Intercept: https://firstlook.org/theintercept/

6. Huffington Post / Education: http://www.huffingtonpost.com/education/

7. Educause: http://www.educause.edu

8. Learning Solutions Magazine: http://www.learningsolutionsmag.com/

9. Ol'Daily: http://www.downes.ca/

10. Instagram: http://instagram.com/

11. Learning Brain: http://www.bioedonline.org/lessons-and-more/resource-collections/the-learning-brain-neuroscience/

12. Fundamentals of Neuroscience course: http://www.mcb80x.org/

13. Wiki focusing on learning theories: http://learningevolves.wikispaces.com/

14. Instructional design: http://edutechwiki.unige.ch/en/Main_Page

15. Blooms digital taxonomy; http://edorigami.wikispaces.com/

16. IRRODL: http://www.irrodl.org/index.php/irrodl

17. New Media Consortium / Horizon Report: http://redarchive.nmc.org/publications

18. Meta glasses: https://www.spaceglasses.com/

19. Google cardboard kits: http://www.hypergridbusiness.com/2014/08/where-to-buy-google-cardboard/

20. xAPI: http://www.adlnet.gov/tla/experience-api/

21. Learning Locker: http://learninglocker.net/

22. http://dl.acm.org/citation.cfm?id=2567574#

23. http://ht.ly/G2ybt

CITATION

de Waard, I. (2015). Tech Dandy, or the Art of Leisure Learning. In: Hopkins, D., ed., *The Really Useful #EdTechBook*, 1st ed. David Hopkins, pp.187-197.

LEARNING TECHNOLOGISTS: CHANGING THE CULTURE OR PREACHING TO THE CONVERTED?

SHARON FLYNN

Assistant Director, Centre for Excellence in Learning and Teaching, at the National University of Ireland, Galway.

@sharonlflynn

http://learntechgalway.blogspot.com

Sharon is Assistant Director at the Centre for Excellence in Learning and Teaching (CELT) at the National University of Ireland Galway. With a background as an academic in computing science, Sharon has a particular interest in technologies for teaching and learning and she leads the Learning Technologies Team at NUI Galway.

INTRODUCTION

The role of a Learning Technologist is varied (Hopkins, 2013), we are involved in lots of different activities, and no two days are ever the same. We are constantly meeting and working with a variety of people, especially those of us who are based in a central unit. In any particular day, we may be involved in meetings, phone calls, online sessions, workshops, seminars, training sessions and events for professional development. But does it ever feel like we are seeing the same faces all the time? When we run events, is it the same reliable few that participate. Are we preaching to the converted?

There is no doubt that Learning Technologists are busy people, but is all our activity making a real difference to the institution as a whole? Is good practice in the use of technology really being embedded in teaching and learning activities.

Are we changing the culture of our institutions?

In this chapter we argue that culture, in different forms, has a significant effect on the work of learning technologists and that it can be a barrier to the adoption of new technologies. We consider the work of the Learning Technologist and what opportunities may exist to change culture. Finally, a case study is presented which attempts to measure the longer term impact of a professional development module in the area of learning technologies, and to answer the question - are we changing a culture or preaching to the converted?

THE SIGNIFICANCE OF CULTURE

Culture can be defined as (from dictionary.com):

> *The sum of attitudes, customs, and beliefs that distinguishes one group of people from another. Culture is transmitted, through language, material objects, ritual, institutions, and art, from one generation to the next.*

When we examine our work as Learning Technologists, and the context within which it takes place, we can see that there are many cultures that affect what we do. Some of those cultures are certainly department/discipline based, where teaching methods and approaches have been passed from generation to generation. *"We teach this way because we've always taught this way"* or *"We teach this way because that's how X is taught"* are common sentiments, if not always expressed explicitly.

The work of a Learning Technologist takes place within a culture - which may vary from discipline to discipline, project to project. Oliver (2010) describes the relationship between an academic and a Learning Technologist, when involved in a collaborative project; initially, the Learning Technologist must understand the context (of the discipline) within which the project is to take place. Oliver notes that *"the academic may realise, through this dialogue, that certain of their take-for-granted practices and values may be culturally determined rather than being general truths"*.

200

There are also institutional cultures at work. For example, my own institution sees itself as research-focussed, and although it states a parity of esteem between research and teaching activities, in practice most academic staff see a clear message that research is more highly valued.

At another level, the economic situation of the country (Ireland), and subsequent government policies, have a significant effect on the culture within the institution. Increased focus on productivity and measurement drives a cultural shift. On the one hand, strategic decisions are taken around the use of technology to increase productivity, which almost always has a negative effect on the environment within which we work. But for those academic staff who are willing to try something new, perhaps to evaluate the use of a new technology, or to work in partnership with the learning technologies team, their efforts are not always recognised or rewarded.

CULTURE AS A BARRIER TO ADOPTING NEW TECHNOLOGIES

Many papers have been written about barriers to adopting technologies for teaching and learning. Reid (2014) provides a review of the literature and identifies five categories for barriers: technology, process, administration, environment, and faculty. On examination, many of the barriers, particularly in the environment category, are a result of departmental or institutional culture.

> *Many faculty members work in a culture that has not included technology in its definition of effective teaching. The institution's culture and norms around instructional technology use are still being formed, and acceptance of use is only gradually growing. (Reid 2014)*

In our experience, the most common reason given by academic staff for not engaging with technology in their teaching is lack of time. Reid (2014) points out that it's not just a matter of time for learning a new technology, but also investment in adapting teaching methods and approaches, reconsidering evaluation, preparing resources and frequent up-skilling can be a disincentive. The culture of a discipline or an institution may determine whether this time and effort is recognised and incentivised. For many staff, it's not clear whether the investment of effort is worthwhile, either to the teaching environment or to their own career progression.

CHANGING A CULTURE?

The title of this chapter asks if we are changing a culture? So then, what is the culture that we might want to change through our work?

I propose that we want to enable and empower staff to use technologies in their teaching and learning. We want to move away from a perception where technology is difficult, time-consuming, of little real value, or unproven. We want to remove perceived barriers, and address real barriers, where we can. Changing a culture takes time.

HOW LEARNING TECHNOLOGISTS MIGHT EFFECT A CHANGE IN CULTURE

Learning Technologists carry out many different types of activities, which can be described as support (reactive), professional development or strategic.

Support activities are often responsive in nature, responding to an email or phone call where the academic (or academic support) has a particular problem and just wants to know how to fix it. Often there is little opportunity for the learning technologist to even understand the context and an immediate response is required.

> *"Sharon, it's that time of year again. I wonder if you could tell me how to move last year's Blackboard stuff into this years?" - email from academic, September 2014*

If, however, the situation is not urgent, and the academic can be persuaded to step back and explain the context and the desired learning outcomes, there can be small opportunities to empower to make a real difference. If the academic has a positive experience through her interactions with the Learning Technologist, this opens the possibilities of being involved in future projects.

Professional development can be through stand-alone seminars and technical training workshops, where the academic, by being present at the event, has already indicated an interest in learning something new. While many staff are satisfied with the skills they pick up on the day, usually sufficient to progress with a technology on a need-to-know basis, others will feel empowered to define a new project based on their new knowledge and may become future collaborators.

Formal, credit-bearing modules offer lots of opportunity. For example, our unit offers a full module (10 ECTS) on Learning Technologies, which is part of a PostGraduate Diploma in Academic Practice. Because participants sign up for a full module, there is more space and time to consider and demonstrate a range of technologies in context.

At the strategic level, our unit actively looks for opportunities to work with a programme, discipline or school on particular topics (e.g. flipped learning, student engagement, plagiarism awareness) where the focus is on the pedagogical context, and a range of technologies relevant to that context can be considered. While Oliver (2010) warns that such projects may not always be successful

> *However, not all projects are successful. One deciding feature seems to be the readiness of the departments involved – the participating academics must already see the need and value of the development, or else they will not engage with it effectively.*

In practice our experience suggests that this approach, coupled with strong leadership within the group, can be very effective.

A NOTE ON CHAMPIONS

As Learning Technologists, we can all identify and describe our technology champions - those members of academic staff who have successfully integrated a particular technology into their teaching, who have evaluated its effectiveness and who are willing to describe and share their experiences. It is certainly true that academics are more likely to engage with technology if it is being promoted by their peers, somebody who is one of their own.

Technology champions are one of the most useful resources that we have, and so it's worth considering exactly what we mean by a "*champion*", and aiming to identify potential champions with a view to developing and supporting them.

A technology champion is certainly somebody who has integrated a particular technology (e.g. flipped learning, clickers, video, podcasts, …) into their teaching, but moreover, somebody who has really considered the pedagogic implications of this. Usually they will have performed some sort of critical evaluation, and be in a position to discuss both the positive and the negative effects. A champion is usually not a technology geek, in fact, the best champions are those who may have been initially sceptical, or certainly have struggled with aspects of the implementation.

In most cases, the use of the technology is evolving or expanding. The champion may have piloted it with a certain group of students and is now considering further rollout, or has seen some opportunity to vary the approach to be more beneficial (to students, to herself, to the discipline or to the institution). Sometimes, having success with one technology will lead to increased confidence to experiment with another.

Most importantly, for Learning Technologists at least, a champion is willing to share her story, not as an expert, but as somebody who tried, who overcame problems, and has had some success. Such people are excellent collaborators and may be persuaded to tell their story beyond the immediate discipline.

With regard to changing a culture, a champion is particularly valuable because they are already part of the culture. They can help to ease a Learning Technologist's initial induction to a particular cultural context, within the practice of legitimate peripheral participation described by Oliver (2010). They can also legitimise the use of a given technology within the culture of a discipline, because they have already demonstrated the value to the discipline.

Finally, in the case where the champion is in a leadership position within a programme or discipline, there can be a very real opportunity to support a change in culture from within.

MEASURING EFFECTIVENESS - A CASE STUDY

How can we tell if we are making a difference? All units within an institution produce annual reports, measuring aspects of their work. For the learning technologies team, we produce metrics such as: how many support tickets were raised; how many workshops and events were run; what was the average attendance at workshops; how many projects completed; how many conference papers given. We can also easily generate information about which disciplines engaged with us the most. While these demonstrate that we were busy, they don't tell us a lot about how effective our work is.

In 2012, we attempted to measure the impact of the Learning Technologies Module, offered as part of the PostGraduate Diploma in Academic Practice and available to academic staff. At the time, we had 4 classes of graduates of the module, almost 40 academics. We wanted to evaluate the longer term effects of the module and measure the impact it was having on the use of technology in teaching at the university. Had we started to address a change of culture, or are we simply supporting those academics who are already technology enthusiasts?

ANALYSING THE PARTICIPANTS

Before we can claim any sort of change in culture, we need to consider the starting point. About 60% of the academics who take this module are taking it as part of the PG Diploma, having completed a PG Certificate in Teaching and Learning in Higher Education. As such they have limited module choice and so it can certainly be argued that they are not necessarily enthusiastic about the topic - just that it was a better choice than something else. The remaining 40% of participants are taking it as a standalone module, and so may be assumed to have a pre-disposition towards technology.

The academics who take this module come from all disciplines across the university, and they have differing levels of comfort with the user of technology. Far from all being technology enthusiasts, we were able to classify the participants by techno-culture (Wheeler 2012). Of the group of 38 graduates of the module, just 2 fell into the definition of **technophile** "*in that they have an affinity with new technology and perceive no particular threat to their way of working, but rather embrace it as a means to enhance or extend their practice*". Even those classified as technophiles admit that they have something to learn. Sample statements from an initial survey of participants include:

> *"I would say that a mixture of inquisitiveness, enthusiasm and willingness to make (silly) mistakes make me one of the early adopters of pretty much every technological development." - Course participant*

> *"Based on my background I don't really have any issues using various new technologies ... I am often one of the first to explore a new technology if only for the fun of it. But when it comes to using it in teaching, I find it really challenging to figure out the most strategically useful way of using a particular technology to achieve a specific learning outcome." - Course participant*

At the other end of the scale, 2 could be described as **technophobic**, those who rarely adopt a new technology.

> *"It just seems alien and the question I keep asking is "Why?? " It seems mad and chaotic. I really do feel I am on a different planet and my hardwiring is different. I was all excited today when reading earlier blogs where it appeared initially that others in the class were the same but then I realized that while you may equate your knowledge with technology to an elementary level I am not even at a preschooler developmental level yet. Lets face it a preschooler can go to the toilet on their own." - Course participant*

The vast majority of our participants can be classified as **technorealists**, those who make deliberate decisions about using technology in teaching and wait until an innovation has been tried and tested. In most cases, these academics will cite lack of time or unclear benefits as reasons for not engaging with technology to date.

> *"In many respects I am somewhat fascinated by new technologies and love to become involved in exploring new methods and ideas. However, I do find I never seem to have either the time or the attention span to become embedded enough to learn the process fully. I tend to learn enough to 'get me by', which sometimes can be more of a hindrance than a help." - Course participant*

We also identified a healthy number of **techno-sceptics** - those who don't lack confidence, but who really question the use of technology at all.

> *"From what I can see, many technologies are created and disseminated primarily for two interrelated purposes – sales and social control. To be honest, I am alarmed that the prevailing view among many is that technologies are largely benign and that it is only the naive who don't appreciate the rules of game. Maybe my anxiety comes from a concern that I simply can't keep up and that I just do not want to admit that to myself or maybe I am turning into a Victor Meldrew before my time. Then again, maybe 'freedom is slavery and ignorance strength' and, I have every reason to be cautious. In summary, I am reasonably confident in learning new technologies, but not at all confident that it is something that I should do in many cases." - Course participant*

Our stated aim within the module is to move each individual participant beyond their comfort zone, to try something new in a supported environment.

ASSESSING THE IMPACT

After 4 years of running the module, we were interested in trying to find out what were the longer term effects of the module and what was the impact on the use of technology in teaching and learning at the institution. We devised a questionnaire that would go out to all previous participants - whether they had successfully completed the module (for credit) or not. We felt strongly that exposure to even some of the elements of the module, without completing the final assessment, could have a positive impact.

Overall we received a 56% response rate, or 22 respondents. The questions were all qualitative, though we were able to derive quantitative data from the results, where useful. Some respondents had completed the module 3 years previously, others had only recently completed. Some had moved on to other institutions, but none had left academia.

In the following narrative, we discuss the survey questions, why we asked them, and the responses we received. Since the survey was qualitative, responses are used to illustrate throughout.

Q.1 Have you continued to use technology in your teaching?
We asked this question to try to understand if the momentum created by the course had continued. Within the module, participants try out a range of technologies, but also have to complete a technology-based project within their own teaching. We wanted to know if they were continuing to innovate within their own area.

Of 22 respondents, just one answered no to this question:

> *"While I did last year during the Diploma course I did not continue doing it this year. This was not due to the lack of interest but rather due to the fact that I have a one year contract so had to prioritise research over teaching. I would use technology again in the future." - Survey respondent*

In this example we can clearly see the effect that the institutional culture has on our work, acting as a barrier.

All other (21) answers listed ways in which innovation in technology use was continuing. For example:

"Using flip cameras to great effect with first years. Have also used Wikis but it wasn't as successful. They tended to work off-line and then submit their work. I use vodcasts to support laboratory work. I have also encouraged postgrad students to use Twitter to follow professional bodies. Generally I've found that students really like activities that support their learning." - Survey respondent

"Yes, I've kept using the blogging thing, and I liked the You Tube and Mp4 bit and am using MP3 audio files extensively to give commentary to students on essays. I have not kept up Twitter but that is just a personal preference." - Survey respondent

Of interest was that in a majority of cases respondents were able to list technologies that hadn't worked for them, as well as those they continued to use. This indicates a certain maturity in use, the ability and confidence to recognise when something isn't working, but not to be discouraged.

Q2. Do you continue to upskill?
We asked this question as an indicator of forward momentum: now that they had achieved something through the module, were they continuing to learn new skills?

Of the 22 responses, 5 indicated that it was too soon - they had only just completed the module. A further 9 people said that they had continued. Of the 8 people who said no, four mentioned time constraints. Others had more considered reasons:

"No. I am 'learning by doing'. I also take advantage of the knowledge of students and alumni." - Survey respondent

"No, but mainly because I feel I have what I need and need to spend time implementing rather than learning more." - Survey respondent

As well as organised workshops for continued professional development, some of the group mentioned less formal approaches:

"I have [continued to upskill] but I find Twitter an excellent resource for updating my skills as participants will highlight learning technology resources. - Survey respondent

The responses to this question were positive, suggesting that participants were self-motivated to continue in formal or informal development and in some cases developing their own Personal Learning Networks (PLNs).

Q3. Have you presented any of your work with technology in education? Have you given a seminar, presented a poster or conference paper, or written an article on your use of technology in teaching? You can include public blogging and other information activities.

This was deliberately left as a very open question, with many possible interpretations. We wanted to know if the participants had felt confident enough to share their work with a group, whether that group be local, discipline-based, or something wider. During the module we had encouraged participants to consider sharing by submitting abstracts to, for example, the annual EdTech conference of the Irish Learning Technology Association (ILTA), which takes place each year.

Of the 22 responses, exactly half indicated that they had presented their work, with 7 having presented at the EdTech conference, which is peer-reviewed. Others mentioned presenting at conferences in their own discipline area.

Four people mentioned less formal presentations within the university such as staff development sessions, while one gave an example of informal presentations:

"Only over coffee with friendly colleagues!" - Survey respondent

A couple of respondents indicated that they had shared their work through blogging, although one suggested that the practice might not be sustainable for her:

"I blogged about my educational practices, including technology, for about

a year. I still think of things I'd like to share, but am starting to suspect that there are more valuable ways of spending my limited time, because doing the blog properly would mean more of a commitment than I feel currently able to give." - Survey respondent

Another respondent suggested that she also used social media to present her work:

"no, although I would occasionally tweet my delight when something makes work more efficient!" - Survey respondent

Three others indicated their intention to present something in the future.

Finally, one participant shared his work, via portfolio, for a prestigious award within his own discipline:

"I was awarded the [XX] prize for teaching and learning and that was based on a Teaching portfolio which I put together following the course. The reviewers noted the use of various technologies and reflection on same. I will probably give a presentation at next year's [XX] conference on my teaching portfolio." - Survey respondent

The answers to this question suggest that the participants put some value on this aspect of their work and are confident and willing to share their expertise with others. Leading on to the next question in the survey, the answers also provide some evidence of emerging champions.

Q4. Are you a technology champion?
We qualified this question with the subquestion: *Have you given advice to colleagues about using technology?* Again, this was a question about willingness to share expertise and experience which could have a wider impact.

Only one person answered in the negative:

> *"No, far from it. More like a technology curmudgeon! But I now know how the various technologies can be used with some discrimination to improve things a bit." - Survey respondent*

In fact, this came from the same person who had been awarded the prize for teaching and learning in his discipline, and could perhaps be classified as a reluctant champion, despite himself.

All the other respondents indicated that they did support others within the discipline, often with improved use of the VLE:

> *"Yes on an ad hoc basis and usually in relation to the use of Blackboard". - Survey respondent*

> *"I offer informal advice to colleagues about ways to customise the VLE to suit their needs." - Survey respondent*

This certainly demonstrates a shift in culture where best use of the VLE is being discussed within a department. It could also indicate less basic support calls to the learning technologies team, prehaps replaced with more sophisticated requests.

Others indicated a wider range of technologies that they support:

> *"Yes. I would be one of the first ports of call in my school regarding problems with clickers and on-line homework." - Survey respondent*

> *"Yes. Blackboard, laptops, Powerpoint-type presentations, video, Twitter, Wordle,..." - Survey respondent*

Some other answers suggest that the respondents may be starting to take on technology leadership roles within the discipline:

> *"Yes, to the extent that my colleagues have swiped my flip cameras!" - Survey respondent*

"I have been showing the staff here how to use Google Earth to its full potential." - Survey respondent

"I am a big fan of technology and try as much as possible to champion it, by increasing the department's visibility on the net and by offering help and support to colleagues." - Survey respondent

We found these responses very encouraging. Not only were people willing to describe themselves as technology champions, but from their descriptions it's clear that discussions around technology use are actually happening within the disciplines, suggesting a shift in culture from within.

Q5. Have you applied for or received funding to support your use of technology?
We asked this question as an indication of innovation with respect to the use of technology in teaching within the discipline. Even the act of making an application for funding, whether successful or not, indicates that institutionally provided resources may not be sufficient and that the person or group making the application is thinking beyond what might be considered conventional for the university.

By applying for research funding around technology, a participant could be moving into the area of scholarship in teaching and learning within their discipline. This area is recognised by the Irish National Forum for the Enhancement of Teaching and Learning in Higher Education as needing to be valued, supported, shared and integrated (National Forum, 2014) and is linked to the culture of the institution. From the report of the National Forum, what is needed to support scholarship in teaching and learning in institutions includes

Recognition of the value of research in teaching and learning both by individual institutions (e.g. in KPIs, promotions, dedicated space, time, providing mentoring) and sectorally. (National Forum, 2013)

Of the 22 responses, 6 indicated that they had applied for funding, and two had been successful. A further two people mentioned their intention to seek funding in the future.

Q6: How did the module help?

As well as asking whether they would recommend the module to colleagues (21 of the 22 respondents said yes, that they had already done so) we also asked how had the module helped with the integration of technologies into their teaching practice.

A number of respondents indicated that it had helped them get started, to overcome an initial reluctance or feeling of being overwhelmed:

> *"I had no previous experience of technology so it assisted in getting me off the ground and braving the world of technologies" - Survey respondent*

> *"To be honest, I don't think I would have experimented with the various learning technologies if I hadn't first been shown them. I feel much more informed now about what is available, and do think that the integration of learning technologies has had a positive impact both on the teaching and hopefully on the learning experience for students." - Survey respondent*

> *"I can't say that it changed my teaching practice but it added to my bag of tricks. I am always willing to try new things. I think that it is good for students to see that effort. It is very good for them to see someone like me (56 years old) who is not afraid to tackle technology. Some of it works, some of it doesn't. It's good for them to see the effort." - Survey respondent*

Others commented that it gave them time and space, or permission, to invest properly in integrating technology:

> *"It made me get around to various things I wanted to do but had not gotten around to doing before!" - Survey respondent*

"The module gave me a mandate to include non-traditional learning methods into my teaching. It also made me think more about the student experience - viewing it from their perspective." - Survey respondent

"To be honest, I don't think I would have experimented with the various learning technologies if I hadn't first been shown them. I feel much more informed now about what is available, and do think that the integration of learning technologies has had a positive impact both on the teaching and hopefully on the learning experience for students." - Survey respondent

"It gave me the support, push and encouragement to try some of the available technologies out there. I believe that these technologies could be used to encourage more students to become 'reflective' and so more engaged and responsible for their own learning and in so doing help them to a deeper understanding of the discipline." - Survey respondent

For one of our original **technophobes**, the experience was transformative:

"The module helped me decide on what would be appropriate to the learning needs of the student cohort I look after. In relation to presenting at a conference about learning technology, it is not something I would have ever have considered myself doing because to be honest I was a techno phobe. Doing the module really helped me get over this. I am not so scared of technology now." - Survey respondent

There was also some evidence that our **technophiles** were beginning to think more deeply about the pedagogical effects of using technology in their teaching.

"I think it had a lot of bearing on my teaching practice as I was already using a lot of technologies. I think it pushed me to reflect on why I was using technologies in teaching. Learning technologies are great and being innovative is great. However I found that the module not only helped me discover new technologies, it made me aware of the need to embed them properly in a curriculum." - Survey respondent

Perhaps the most challenging participant in a group is the **techno-sceptic**, but who can also bring a wonderful balance to the class. The **techno-sceptics** can help to ground the group.

> *"The module allowed a discussion of where trends were going and there was some space for grumpy types to make observations about why we should bother using the various tech and how and to what purpose. However, we were then cast into the pit of actually having to do something......and that was fun and more or less got one to understand the basics of 'how to'." - Survey respondent*

From the responses to this question, we could see that the module, with its mix of theory and practice, with plenty of opportunity for discussion and exploration of themes, supports different types in different ways. While respecting the backgrounds techno-cultures of the various participants, through a supportive environment, each individual can be encouraged to try something new and progress in his own disciplinary context.

Overall, we conclude that the answers to the survey indicate that there is a small shift in culture happening, though it will take time to see the benefits of this. There are indications that the module is helping to create champions, people who are willing to share their experiences and to spread the word. There is evidence that good practice in the use of technology is being embedded in teaching and learning activities. Finally, it is clear that, through the module, we are not just supporting technology enthusiasts, but also empowering more reluctant academics.

REFERENCES

Hopkins, D. (2013). What is a Learning Technologist?. 1st ed.

ILTA, Irish Learning Technology Association. http://ilta.ie/ [Accessed 25.11.2014]

National Forum for the Enhancement of Teaching and Learning in Higher Education (2013) "Summary Report of Sectoral Dialogue Sessions in Irish Higher Education, November - December 2013". Available from http://teachingandlearning.ie/wp-content/uploads/2014/03/Sectoral-Report.pdf [Accessed 21.12.2014]

Oliver, M. (2010) "What do Learning Technologists do?". Innovations in Education and Teaching International, 39(4), pp. 245-252.

Reid, P. (2014) "Categories for barriers to adoption of instructional technologies". Education and Information Technologies, 19(2), pp 383-407.

Wheeler, S. New ideas in a digital age. http://steve-wheeler.blogspot.ie/2012/03/new-ideas-in-digital-age.html [Accessed 25.11.2014]

CITATION

Flynn, S. (2015). Learning Technologists: Changing the culture or preaching to the converted?. In: Hopkins, D., ed., *The Really Useful #EdTechBook*, 1st ed. David Hopkins, pp.199-217.

THIS IS YOUR FIVE-MINUTE WARNING!

MIKE MCSHARRY

Company Owner, Systems and Education Limited

@mikemcsharry

http://www.systemed.co.uk/

Mike has been working in the IT industry since 1980 when he was introduced to a computer terminal in Land Rover. Since 1996 his main business has been closely linked to primary education. Since then he's seen the explosion of computing in primary schools overseen by various government initiatives and agencies. Mike is keen to help teachers enjoy using the technologies available in creative and effective ways.

WHAT IF MICHAEL GOVE *(1)* WAS RIGHT?

What if the wholesale demolition and rebuilding of the primary school curriculum really is the best thing to ever happen? The curriculum changes were dramatic and included a new discrete subject: computing. This introduced concepts such as "*algorithms... unambiguous instructions ... and logical thinking*" to even the youngest of school pupils. *(2)*

What if the introduction of computational thinking to 4 year olds really does make a generation of analytical, probing young people? What if all this happens?

If this happens then these young people will be entering our colleges and universities in 14 years. Perhaps this is the five-minute warning for Further and Higher Education?

The likelihood of the current curriculum being around for more than 5 years is probably very remote; it feels as if every Secretary of State has an uncontrollable urge to tamper with that which came before. Even allowing for this we will see perhaps four cohorts of children who will have received some grounding in computing skills. This grounding may set them up for life.

The following quote from Douglas Adams *(3)* could probably be revised quite dramatically.

> *"I've come up with a set of rules that describe our reactions to technologies:*
>
> *1. Anything that is in the world when you're born is normal and ordinary and is just a natural part of the way the world works.*
>
> *2. Anything that's invented between when you're fifteen and thirty-five is new and exciting and revolutionary and you can probably get a career in it.*
>
> *3. Anything invented after you're thirty-five is against the natural order of things."*

Before the age of 35 it's very likely that our current young pupils will see five or six complete cycles of invention and obsolescence in most spheres of their life. My own experience with technology is an example: within 30 years data storage on home computers has gone from cassette tape, via floppy disks of various sizes, through hard disks and CD-ROMs, to rewritable DVDs, USB devices and on to cloud storage.

Within 20 years Kodak has gone from being one of the world's largest user of silver to an organisation clinging on to existence. The reducing demands for silver were highlighted by the Silver Users Association in their report in 2004 *(4)*. This was further emphasised by the Silver Institute's report in 2012 *(5)*. In a strange twist, photographic film is being replaced by photocells as a major industry for silver.

In some areas of the country children are starting at school very poorly prepared for life. Their very first experience of being taught to think is from their teachers. Perhaps we should add the following step to the quote from Douglas Adams *(3)*

> *"1.5. Anything that I learn in my first year at school will guide my approach*

to life."

NEW CURRICULUM

There are a number of challenges facing schools now, December 2014:

- *Teachers in primary schools are in a bind.* They are expected to teach something they have never learned.
- *The skills gap between what teachers think they know and what they are expected to teach is enormous.* The perception of the spread of computing and technical skills across teaching cohorts is often wide of the mark.
- *There is a perception that newer, younger teachers are more computer literate than older or more experienced teachers.* In reality many of the newer, younger teachers are very comfortable with using the parts of technology they need and want. Expertise in Word, PowerPoint, Facebook, Instagram and Amazon isn't really going to help them teach coding and computational skills.

Surprisingly, teachers who joined in with the introduction of 'floor roamers' *(6)* (they're the big ones in the stockroom with the flat batteries) and the many flavours of Logo *(7)* are probably better skilled up to work with this computing curriculum. As I write this paper, my Twitter stream includes some heated discussion on the suitability of something as 'so last week' as Logo in the teaching of computing skills. In primary school staff trainings I conducted in the first few days of the new computing curriculum, we used Logo as a welcome, familiar starting point for the teacher groups.

There is a massive opportunity for school leaders to tap into the skills latent in their teaching workforce. Remember, educe is the root word of educate:

Educe – Bring out or develop something latent or potential

A simple programming tool called Scratch *(8)* was introduced to many decision makers and influencers as the new curriculum was being introduced. This tool allows children to quickly construct, run and understand computing in a safe and fun environment. At the "Barefoot Computing at Schools" launch in July 2014, in a live web link, Mitch Resnick, the Scratch developer, said "*Learning to code is coding to leam*".

The analytical and problem solving skills young people can develop using simple tools can be, and are being, quickly and easily transferred to other subject areas.

The primary school curriculum, introduced in September 2014, can be interpreted to show all subjects being taught discretely. Many schools are already looking at how tools and ideas can be used across the curriculum. Data handling, being used in science, and computer programming tools, being used in geography, are simple examples already being used in schools now. The linkages in simple robots can introduce skeletal concepts and ideas to help with early Key Stage 2 Science *(9)*. Building the same robot and actually programming it helps to bring the Key Stage 2 Design and Technology curriculum *(10)* to life.

Software developers have been making exciting, icon-driven solutions aimed at all abilities. This means that coding and computing principles are being introduced to the very youngest pupils and those children who struggle to read or are currently finding English difficult. Tablet devices offer a way for pupils to learn individually and some pupils are grasping coding principles before they can read quite straightforward English. The personal space offered by a tablet device provides pupils of all abilities opportunities to use these packages in a non-threatening environment.

The infrastructure challenges in schools need careful consideration. At the Future of Technology in Education (FOTE) 2010 conference at the University of London Jeremy Speller *(11)*, from the University Computing Centre, explained how he had designed a lecture theatre based on students needing to use their own laptops. The theatre was duly kitted out with plenty of power and data sockets. The students then turned up with tablet (Wi-Fi enabled) devices and were desperate for quality wireless coverage. There are equivalent challenges facing schools and universities today. It is important to recognise these challenges and plan the appropriate action.

Budget constraints tied to individual learning targets are showing that "Bring Your Own Device" (BYOD) could offer many benefits to schools. If not handled correctly these devices, which are not under the full control of school networks could introduce severe virus and hacking problems. Correct and well thought out measures are needed to be put in place to ensure flexibility does not spell disaster.

The march of technology is relentless. Andrew S Grove, the late CEO of Intel Corporation once said "*Whatever can be done with technology, will be done*" (12). That phrase could be rewritten as "*whatever can be done with technology, will be done … far faster and far cheaper than you can imagine*".

We take the rate of change for granted. In the summer of 2014 I heard two retired ladies in a pub extolling the virtues of their camera phones, rather loudly. One lady had used her phone to take a picture of her new grandson and then pop it on FaceBook. This allowed her other son in Australia to see his new nephew within the first few days of his life. The response from her friend was terrific.

> "*We used to take a photo, and possibly a second for good measure. We'd wait until the film was finished then take it to the chemists. We'd get them back within the week. Hopefully, one of the pictures was good enough to pop back in for a few extra prints. That normally took another week. Then we'd post it. I never sent photos Air-Mail, they were far too expensive. They'd be lucky to see pictures before the babies were 6 months old.*"

CHALLENGES

Imagine this: a small handheld device. This device uses induction charging. This device has three-axis gyro controlled motors. This device is controlled from a tablet or smartphone, without using the school wireless network. This device has free Apps available which together cover nearly all aspects of the primary curriculum. In real terms this device costs less money than a box of 5¼" floppy disks (see Footnote).

Imagine no more, these are already in use in St Patricks Catholic Primary School, Leicester. The effect of the introductory training session was so powerful that early years teachers came back at 4PM for more training ideas. *(13)*

Schools are about to face a challenge with the computing curriculum, which is only very slowly being recognised. As I've already highlighted, in autumn 2014 primary schools are introducing computing across all year groups. With a few exceptions this roll out is to a base level of zero for every year group. In effect, everything learnt by the pupils is new. The current Year 6 pupils will hopefully be taught at a level higher than their colleagues in year 5. Next year, the year 6 pupils will no longer be coming from a base level of zero. Is the curriculum for year 6 next year a beneficial step up from year 5?

Move the clock forward. The current Year 3 pupils will have had four years of computing teaching and learning by the time they reach secondary school. Hopefully, each year will show significant progression. This means that these pupils will be entering secondary schools with a level of computing and analytical skills so far ahead of the pupil currently entering secondary schools.

As a parent of children who have gone through the primary / secondary transition I have first-hand experience of this infamous dip. The dip may become significantly deeper. What will the effect be of these pupils in Year 7.

Primary schools are different from secondary schools. One difference is that one teacher works through all subjects with pupils. The analytical and questioning skills will be developed and, hopefully, welcomed in all the subject areas in the primary classroom.

This chapter is being written in late October 2014. Primary schools have only had one half term of the new curriculum. Already in primary schools I have seen examples of the computing curriculum being enthusiastically taken into other subject areas.

Amongst the curriculum changes introduced in September 2014 the primary history curriculum was completely revised *(14)*. This introduced the need to study Ancient Greek Life. One of the often used stories from Ancient Greece is the story of the terrible monster, the Minotaur *(15)*. One primary school teacher is setting a task for her pupils using the labyrinth as a background for Scratch and making the Minotaur into a sprite. The pupils will have to write the code to get Minotaur out of the Labyrinth.

In June 2010, Kodu was launched at the Computing at Schools conference in Birmingham *(16 and 17)*. This visual programming language is free of charge and has been used by primary school and secondary school children in many areas of the curriculum.

Are the secondary school subject teachers ready for these analytical, questioning pupils that are about to appear in their Year 7s? Are the subject specialists in the secondary schools even aware of this?

Already, we have heard examples of this from primary school head teachers. The timescales on the following event are quite frightening.

During the summer holidays, August 2014, my team prepared software and networks in a number of primary schools. This work allowed the new curriculum to be rolled out smoothly and easily from a teaching and learning perspective. On August 28th, 2014, we ran a half-day inset day in one of the primaries and introduced a few key elements of one of the packages they had chosen, Scratch. During the inset session staff admitted to knowing of Scratch but never having used it.

In mid-September the head teacher visited one of the secondary schools with a small group of Year 6 pupils for a secondary school open day. The computing subject leader took the pupils into an IT suite and explained a little about this new software they were rolling out in the school. Scratch. Sadly, no photos or recordings were taken of the computing leaders' reactions when these pupils immediately changed backgrounds, characters and then threw some code around.

225

This chapter started with a five-minute warning for Further and Higher Education. Perhaps Secondary Education is already working through the one-minute warning?

SUMMARY

The future belongs to those who are willing to learn and tackle new challenges. I've learned so much in the last 30 years - and learned that there's still such a lot to find out.

FOOTNOTE:

5¼ " Floppy Disc (18)	$4.95
5¼" Floppy Disc (box of 10)	$49.50

Equivalent price in £ Sterling (19)

5¼" Floppy Disc	£2.05
5¼" Floppy Disc (box of 10)	£20.54

Adjusting for inflation (Browning) (20):
£1.00 in 1980 is worth £4.42 in 2014

The current real value of a box of ten 5¼" floppy discs in 1980, roughly 1.2MB each (21) taking inflation into account, is £90.78, equates to roughly £7.57 per MB.

NOTES

1.   Michael Gove. Secretary of State for Education in England and Wales, 2010 to 2014
     http://en.wikipedia.org/wiki/Michael_Gove

2.   National Curriculum Computing Programs of Study Key Stage 1 and 2
     https://www.gov.uk/government/uploads/system/uploads/attachment_data/file/239033/PRI

MARY_national_curriculum_-_Computing.pdf

3. Adams, D. (2002). The Salmon of Doubt. New York: Harmony Books.

4. Silver Users Association (2004)
    http://www.silverusersassociation.org/silver/demand.shtml

5. The Silver Institute (2011) https://www.silverinstitute.org/site/wp-content/uploads/2011/07/futuresilverindustrialdemand.pdf

6. Floor roamers are educational robots - the manufacturers information is here
    http://www.valiant-technology.com/uk/pages/what_is_roamer.php?cat=8id0

7. Logo, a programming language, was devised by Seymour Papert. Information on Papert's ideas can be found here http://www.papert.org/

8. With Scratch, you can program your own interactive stories (http://scratch.mit.edu)

9. National Curriculum Science Programs of Study Key Stage 1 and 2
    https://www.gov.uk/government/uploads/system/uploads/attachment_data/file/286349/Primary_science_curriculum_to_July_2015_RS.pdf

10. National Curriculum Design and Technology Programs of Study Key Stage 1 and 2
    https://www.gov.uk/government/uploads/system/uploads/attachment_data/file/239041/PRIMARY_national_curriculum_-_Design_and_technology.pdf

11. Jeremy Speller - The Mobile University: last years' model?
    https://www.youtube.com/watch?v=cSWVPNxZHoY

12. Grove, Andrew S (1996) Only the Paranoid Survive - How to Exploit the Crisis Points that Challenge Every Company and Career Profile Books Limited

13. Using Snakes and Ladders to teach the primary computing curriculum
    http://www.systemed.co.uk/snakes-and-ladders/

14. National Curriculum History Programs of Study Key Stage 1 and 2
    https://www.gov.uk/government/uploads/system/uploads/attachment_data/file/239035/PRIMARY_national_curriculum_-_History.pdf

15. The story of the labyrinth and th minotaur - Ancient Greece for Kids
    http://greece.mrdonn.org/theseus.html

16. Introduction of Kodu http://www.mikemcsharry.com/2010/07/kodu/

17. Kodu Web Site http://www.kodugamelab.com/

18. 1980 Radio Shack Catalog Low-res page 171 of 176.
    http://www.radioshackcatalogs.com/html/1980/h171.html

19. Graph of £/$ exchange rate (1971 - today). http://www.miketodd.net/encyc/dollhist-graph2.htm

20. Historic inflation calculator: how the value of money has changed since 1900.

http://www.thisismoney.co.uk/money/bills/article-1633409/Historic-inflation-calculator-value-money-changed-1900.html

21.   Floppy disk. http://en.wikipedia.org/wiki/Floppy_disk

CITATION

McSharry, M. (2015). This is your five-minute warning. In: Hopkins, D., ed., The Really Useful #EdTechBook, 1st ed. David Hopkins, pp.219-228.

POSTSCRIPT: WHAT, OR WHERE NEXT?

DAVID HOPKINS

"Every book represents a moment when someone sat quietly - and that quiet is part of the miracle, make no mistake - and tried to tell us the rest of the story." J. R. Moehringer

Christmas, 2014. As I sit at my kitchen table I have several different formats of this book in front of me –draft of the printed edition, my Kindle, my iPad, my laptop, and my iPhone –showing me how the same paragraph or table or image or section reads. I got the idea from Zak in one of his blog posts (1). Make no mistake; there are differences, some quite large, between how each platform displays the same information from the same source. Getting the eBooks to work across the different formats (EPUB and MOBI) and different platforms (tablet, smartphone, laptop, desktop) is hard work.

I am in awe of what we have been able to achieve here. Not only have a group of incredibly busy and hard working people been able to come together on a shared passion - our work and those we work with - but we've all been able to share the journey with our colleagues, friends, and family too.

Let's not forget that, in the time it took from my first tentative emails to each chapter author, we've had two births and one wedding, and a whole lot of emails, tweets, DMs, meet-ups (and tweet-ups), events & conferences attended. Congratulations to Zak and his wife for the birth of their first daughter Ava, and to Peter and wife for, not only their Las Vegas wedding (love the photos!), but also the birth of their son, Maximilus! I am happy and proud that both new Dads' have been able to fit this book into their new, very different and very busy schedules.

The biggest thank you goes out to all of you that are reading this book. It has been an idea I'd toyed with for a while but took time and a whole heap of courage to broach the subject with a few trusted and close friends before I realised there may be scope and a market for it. Even then it took me a while before I sent the initial invites to people who I thought had both something to say and (hopefully) the time to say it. The concept of personal, reflective, and relevant journeys or stories in a field of expertise is not new, but not one I've seen encompassing and embracing the world of educational technology from such a wide range of practitioners and researchers. I only wish we could have had more people writing and collaborating on it. Perhaps a second edition?

I am not someone who likes to shout about what I do or how I do it, despite my blog having over 800 posts, between 6,000 and 10,000 unique visitors each month, and being followed by nearly 8,000 people on Twitter. These are, I've been told, good stats to boast about. I have used both Twitter and my blog, among others, as a focal point for my own thoughts, reflections, readings, research, communications, collaborations, friends, colleagues, and general ramblings. These interactions have helped me learn more about my job(s), my employers, my colleagues, my peers, my interests, and my own belief in trying to use different technologies (as well as the different approaches to the same old technologies) to better the students' learning experience, or to make the classroom or lecture theatre a more interesting place to work. In doing so I too have been learning, as I said, more about me and what I like to learn about.

When I started this project I didn't know what it would look like at this point, on the last few pages – I had a better idea on what the cover would look like than the contents! I had an idea on who I'd like to help me write it, but not what they would want to write about. Emails and edits to various Google Docs over the period of July 2014 to now has seen very different writing styles and very different perspectives coming to the fore. Tying to see how everyone can be accommodated and fit together in one cohesive volume, whilst retaining their own individual style and approach, is not easy.

This so easily could have been a book about learning technology and Higher Education, but I wouldn't want to read that either, which is why invites were sent to friends and colleagues from other areas of my networks: Further Education, workplace learning, museums, corporate eLearning, etc. It is unfortunate that work and personal circumstances meant some stories and some chapters were unable to be included.

I want to highlight, in these last few words, some key moments in the process of collating and editing the book. I would never have learned so much about the historical journey(s) of technology and education as we have from Lesley (Price) if I hadn't asked her to be involved. I learnt from Mike (McShary) about the state of primary education and their computing / network needs in Leicestershire: when primary school children show teachers from the secondary school they're about to go to, just what they can (already) do with PowerPoint or Word... only for those teachers to announce in shocked monotone that they now understand why their own IT classes are so badly attended. Their own students have been doing that for years, and need something different to 'click here to save your document'! I hope Mike writes more about this at some point as there are so many lessons to be learned (and from Lesley's experience too) which can help build stronger and more effective learning environments for the young as they progress through the education system.

Without this book perhaps some of these stories may never have seen the light of day? I am certain there are many more stories out there that not only highlight what we're missing or doing wrong or don't understand properly, just as there are numerous examples of what we are doing right, where we have made a difference in just one child or one class or one school.

Please share your stories. With me. With each other. With anyone who'll listen.

Use the #EdTechBook hashtag on social networks, with your Personal Learning Network (PLN), on your blog, or even on someone else's blog. This book isn't the start of anything new ... but it could be a further catalyst to improve the use of technology for learning (all aspects of learning, in all possible locations), to highlight 'bad' practices and to investigate new ones.

Please also leave a comment or review on the page where you bought or downloaded this book from. This is one small step that will bring the #EdTechBook community to the attention of your PLN and your peers. The next is, as I've already said, to share your story. Do it!

Thank you.

NOTES

1. Zak Mensah eBook testing kit: http://www.zakmensah.co.uk/2012/10/16/under-the-cover-of-the-mrc-ebook/

ABOUT DAVID HOPKINS

Before becoming a Learning Technologist in 2007 I progressed through a couple of 'careers' after graduating from Kingston University: a degree in Geology served me well for a few years in the oil & gas industry in London and Reading, and Internet development and communications across the south coast of England. But it wasn't until I joined the Business School at Bournemouth University that I began to learn about learning, about being a Learning Technologist, and supporting distance learning students and a fully-online degree. It was here I developed my understanding about learning technology, and the fact that there was so much I didn't know, and started on my journey to find out 'what is a Learning Technologist?'

Eight years later, and now at Warwick Business School and Warwick University, I am still asking the same questions, finding the same difficulties in different systems, different tools, and different meetings. Not everything is the same, but much of the issues I've faced, and others around me too, are still here and still being addressed. Much of the technology on my desk or in my pocket is radically different and markedly more powerful than when I started this journey. But we are still searching for answers on how we use it 'appropriately' and in a 'considered' manner to enhance, not detract, from the purpose of its intent– namely, for learning.

BOOKS ALSO BY DAVID HOPKINS

QR Codes in Education, 2013   What is a Learning Technologist? 2013

14247454R00134

Printed in Poland
by Amazon Fulfillment
Poland Sp. z o.o., Wrocław